# CONTENTS

*Growing annuals*    5

• What are annuals? • Hardy annuals • Half-hardy annuals
• Hardy biennials • Buying seeds • Seed packets • Young plants
• What can go wrong? • Annuals in containers • Sowing annuals
• Soil preparation • Thinning out • Growing on • Hardening off
• Planting • Watering • Feeding

*Using annuals in your garden*    10

• Bedding schemes • Hardy annual schemes • Care-free hardy
annuals • Border fillers

*Popular annuals*    12

• A–Z of 90 popular annuals from abutilon to zinnia

*Annuals for cutting*    103

• Picking flowers • Buying cut flowers • Hygiene
• Clean water and 'flower food' • Arranging flowers
• Making the most of your cut flowers

*Flowering chart*    106

*Index*    108

*Acknowledgments*    112

## KEY TO AT A GLANCE TABLES

SOWING/PLANTING    FLOWERING

At a glance tables are your quick guide.
For full information, consult the accompanying text.

*LEFT: Dwarf zinnias are planted in bold groups amongst the mauve,
pink and white flowers of petunias.*

*ABOVE: The two-lipped shape of an old-fashioned snapdragon.
When squeezed at the sides the flowers 'snap' open and closed.*

# GROWING ANNUALS

*Annuals are perhaps the easiest plants you will ever grow. Yet their ease of growth in no way detracts from their ability to provide colour in the garden, in some cases virtually all-year-round. Whether your garden is large, small, or you work within the confines of just a small patio, annuals are plants for you.*

Miracles are happening in our gardens every day, but perhaps the greatest 'miracle' in which we can take part is growing plants from seeds. Nothing is quite as amazing, or as humbling, as seeing a fully-grown plant, which started life as a tiny seed, burst into flower and create a riot of colour just a few months after it was sown. Some annuals need no more care than simply scattering the seeds over the surface of the ground and 'raking' them in using your fingertips – others demand only that they are sown to the correct depth and then given room to grow as they develop. By their very nature, many annuals produce brilliant results even in the poorest of soils. So get some seed catalogues, visit the local garden centre, and start performing your own garden miracles with the easiest plants on earth!

*LEFT: Annuals like these purple violas and white-flowered lobularia (alyssum) can be sown directly into the soil where you want them to flower, in criss-crossing patterns as here.*

*ABOVE: Rudbeckia or coneflower is available in a wide range of sizes, and provides valuable colour in late summer.*

*MANY ANNUALS THRIVE in some of the most inhospitable parts of the garden. These portulacas or sun flowers are perfectly at home growing on a rockery with very little soil for their roots – they are just as suited to light, sandy soils and make good summer bedding plants.*

## WHAT ARE ANNUALS?

Virtually all annuals are raised by sowing seeds, either in early spring under cover (in a heated greenhouse, conservatory or on the kitchen windowsill), or directly into prepared soil outdoors. Some annuals are so adaptable that you only need sow them once – from then on these so-called 'self-seeders' regularly drop seeds into the soil which then 'come up', or germinate, of their own accord. In many ways these 'hardy annuals' do a better job at sowing than we do – finding just the right spot for perfect growth – often in places we might never dream of actually sowing seeds, such as between the cracks in paving stones and in the gravel of driveways.

At the other extreme are annuals which need to be started into growth long before the warmer days of spring arrive outdoors. The so-called 'half-hardy' annuals are those plants which are damaged by frosts, but which perform brilliantly during the summer months. For these you must be able to provide suitable growing conditions, especially at sowing time, when temperature is all-important for actually getting the seeds to come up. In some cases, such as with ricinus, the castor oil plant, it is grown as a half-hardy annual, even though it is by nature a shrub, which in its native habitat would, like the shrubs in our gardens, eventually form a large plant. Petunias are another example of a half-hardy annual which is really a perennial plant, and quite capable of surviving the winter if potted-up and kept protected in a cold but 'frost-free' place overwinter. It helps to understand what the terms mean when growing annuals as you will come across them all the time in catalogues and on the back of seed packets.

## HARDY ANNUALS

The easiest of all annuals to grow, sow hardy annuals exactly where you want the plants to flower. Many hardy annuals do not like root disturbance, so bear this in mind.

They are given their ideal planting distances by gradually 'thinning out' as the young plants grow – all this means is carefully removing a few plants every few weeks in spring, to give those left behind more room to develop. By early summer this thinning should be complete, and plants can be left to produce flowers. Hardy annuals are not affected by low temperatures, and many, like calendula, the pot marigold, are sown and germinate outdoors in September for strong plants with earlier flowers the following spring. Most self-seeders belong to this group.

## HALF-HARDY ANNUALS

As already mentioned, these plants are not able to withstand frost or freezing temperatures and must be raised from seed every season, often starting in late winter and very early spring. Many half-hardy annuals are actually 'perennials' – plants which keep growing year after year, but which are better-suited to our needs when grown as strong, young plants every season. Half-hardy annuals are only planted (or moved outdoors if grown in containers) when spring frosts are finished. The exact timing of this depends on the actual area you garden in, but this book gives sowing/planting times for average conditions in the middle of Britain. At the other end of the season, the first autumn frosts will flatten most half-hardy annuals, and they can be removed for composting.

## HARDY BIENNIALS

A biennial is simply a plant which straddles two growing seasons before it produces its show of flowers or foliage. A good example is cheiranthus, or wallflower, which is sown outdoors in early summer. The young leafy plants are grown on, then lifted and planted in October where you want flowers the following spring. Think of hardy biennials as annuals with a 'foot' in two seasons – instead of producing their flowers or leaves all within what we think of as 'summer', they get going in one season, spend the winter building up speed, then go all out for flowering the next spring and summer. Biennials are especially useful for filling any 'gaps' between late spring and early summer, and many such as sweet William are easy and worthwhile plants for cut flowers.

## BUYING SEEDS

Growing from seed is addictive – once you have sampled one seed catalogue you will certainly want more. You can buy annual seeds by sending for them by post or a home delivery service, by visiting garden centres or the gardening section of do-it-yourself stores, or, increasingly, by buying them with your other shopping at the supermarket.

The choice will always be greater in catalogues, but the more limited range that you might find in garden centres can actually be more helpful. The seed packets here are guaranteed to be colourful, giving encouragement to the beginner. Some mail order seed companies pack in plain, information-only packets for mail order – this is no reflection on the quality of the seeds, but they do lack inspiration! Bright, colourful packets are a great help when planning a colour-themed display with annuals, so do not be afraid to play around with a handful of packets until you get a good balance or contrast of colours just to your liking.

If you do buy seeds from garden centres and similar outlets, always avoid any packets that are faded, yellow, and have obviously been exposed to the sun, as the results are likely to be disappointing.

## SEED PACKETS

Remember that seeds are alive, and need looking after to keep them in tip-top condition until sowing. Inside most seed packets you will find another, smaller packet made of foil. Seeds are sealed inside this inner packet in a kind of 'suspended animation' which preserves them until the foil seal is broken. This is when the normal ageing processes of the seed begins. Where this type of storage is not vital for success, seeds are simply found sealed within the outer paper packet. Foil packets should not be opened until the time of sowing for best results. On most packets the inspiration on the front is backed-up by full growing instructions on the reverse. The better packets give sowing times, expected flowering period, and alternative sowing times in autumn. Keep seed packets after sowing – along with catalogues they build up into an invaluable reference library which you can refer to as and when necessary. Always keep seeds in a cool, dry, frost-free place.

## YOUNG PLANTS

Many half-hardy annuals included in this book can also be bought in spring and summer as 'young plants', and this is stated, where relevant, in the paragraph 'features' for each of the 90 annuals covered. The term 'young plant' covers anything from ready-germinated trays of small seedlings to a large plant, perhaps in flower, growing in a 9cm (3½in) pot which you will find for sale in garden centres. Buying young plants simply means that a lot of the work in raising the plants from seed has been done for you by the grower – which has advantages and disadvantages. Young plants are a great help if you do not have facilities for raising seeds or enough space, and they are often delivered ready to go straight into containers. The range compared to the number of varieties available from seed is limited, although this is always improving. You pay for convenience – seed raising is usually cheaper than buying in young plants.

# WHAT CAN GO WRONG?

## Yellow leaves
● Seedlings are being grown too cold in the early stages or plants may have been planted outdoors too early.
● Plants may need feeding – water thoroughly with an all-purpose liquid or soluble plant food, wetting the leaves at the same time to act as a foliar feed.

## Curled or distorted leaves
● Look for clusters of aphids attacking flower buds and the youngest leaves at the shoot tips. Rub them off with your fingers or use a spray containing permethrin.
● Drift from weedkillers can cause this problem, so take great care if you are treating a lawn for weeds using a hormone weedkiller – avoid days when there is any breeze, and keep well away from bedding displays.

## Holes and silvery trails on/in leaves
● Slugs and snails will eat most annual plants and are a particular threat in late spring and early summer, especially after rain when the air is warm and moist. They leave silver slime-trails on the soil and on plants where they have been feeding. Chemical slug pellets can be scattered sparingly among plants or an unbroken ring of sharp grit 5cm (2in) wide can be used as a physical deterrent on smaller areas. Another option is to check plants at night and pick off slugs and snails while they feed, dropping them into salty water.

## White 'powder' on leaves
● Powdery mildew affects many annuals but not usually until late summer. This disease is not a serious threat and treatment is not needed.

## Seedlings indoors suddenly collapse and fall over
● 'Damping off' disease can attack annual seedlings, and is a particular problem if the compost becomes too wet. Always use clean pots for sowing and fresh compost. If it does attack, water lightly with a copper-based fungicide and resow to play safe.

## Leaf edges chewed
● Various caterpillars will attack annuals and can soon strip leaves bare. Pick them off by hand or use a spray containing permethrin, wetting both sides of the leaves with a strong jet from the sprayer.

## Plants cut off at ground level
● Cutworms can sever newly planted bedding plants outdoors causing a sudden wilting and yellowing of plants under attack. Search around in the soil and the greenish-brown caterpillars are easily found and destroyed.

## Creamy-white grubs eating roots
● Vine weevil grubs can cause severe damage to container plants. Never re-use old compost, and if you find grubs, treat all pots with biological control or a chemical based on phenols as a drench.

*Orange marigolds, red and orange nasturtiums, asters and brown-coned rudbeckia intermingle forming a colour co-ordinated annual border.*

One of the wisest approaches is to decide carefully just what you feel you can achieve with your existing facilities. If your 'propagator' (somewhere that plants are raised from seeds in the early stages) is just the kitchen windowsill, then buying half-hardy annuals in as young plants might be the best option. These small plug plants are delivered in mid-spring and can be potted up and grown on on the windowsill or even next to the glass in an unheated conservatory. This cuts out the often tricky job of germinating the seeds to begin with, but means you can still grow the plants you really want. And of course there is nothing to stop you sowing hardy annuals straight into the soil outdoors at the right time.

If you are more restricted, say to just a small patio or balcony, young plants might be the whole solution – larger plants are delivered (or can be bought) in late spring and early summer and these can be planted straight into containers and hanging baskets without growing on. Even then there is nothing to stop you scattering a few seeds of malcolmia, Virginian stock, in the top of your patio pots for some quick and scented flowers!

Most seed catalogues and specialist young plant suppliers carry extensive and informative sections on young plants, and they are well worth getting hold of. Pay particular attention to 'last order dates' – these are the cut-off points for placing young plant orders and many start to appear even as early as January and February.

## ANNUALS IN CONTAINERS

A container in the broadest gardening sense is anything capable of holding compost and supporting plant growth –

this could be a 9cm (3½in) diameter plastic plant pot to a large terracotta trough or tub. Whatever you use, it must have some form of drainage, and this is usually through holes in the base. Moulded plastic containers often have no preformed holes and so you must drill these before planting up. Waterlogged compost kills plant roots and the whole plant will soon die.

For most purposes a good 'multipurpose' compost serves all of an annual plant's needs – from sowing to growing on and finally being planted up. Most multipurpose composts are based on peat with plant nutrients and other materials such as water-storing granules and 'wetters' (allowing dried-out compost to be re-wetted) already added. An increasing number of composts available are based on recycled materials, and the coir-based ones are improving constantly. A few specific plants do prefer a soil-based compost, such as the 'John Innes' types, both for sowing and growing – details of these are given under 'growing method' where relevant. Always buy fresh bags of compost in spring, avoiding any that are over-heavy and wet, or split with green algae growing in them, or faded and past their sell-by date!

There is no reason why hardy annuals cannot be used for container growing – the fact that many are usually sown direct into the soil is not a problem. Simply sow them in small pots or multi-cell trays (plastic trays where the area is divided into individual units or 'cells') at the same times as recommended for outdoor sowing, and plant into your containers during spring. Where appropriate under each plant entry, varieties suited to containers are given – these are usually dwarfer versions of taller varieties, and the range is increasing all the time. Half-hardy annuals offer great scope for container growing, for the reasons already discussed.

## SOWING ANNUALS

Annual seeds are either sown indoors or outdoors. Those sown outdoors are the easiest – they need no extra warmth or heat, just sow them in a patch of well-prepared ground and thin to give them space as they grow. Sowing depth will depend on the size of the seed, but it is essential to work the soil using a rake (or your fingers in a small area) so it is fine and crumbly to at least 2.5cm (1in) deep.

Seed can then be simply scattered over the soil and raked in, or sown in seed drills – these are simply grooves made in the soil with the head of a rake, the edge of a piece of wood, a length of bamboo cane or even the side of your hand. Whichever you use, just press the edge into the soil to make a groove of the right depth. Then sprinkle the seeds thinly along the drill, by rubbing them between your finger and thumb. Once finished, soil is moved back over the seeds with a rake or by lightly brushing the flat of your hand over the sown area. Take care not to disturb the sown seeds, and label with the variety and date sown. If you are sowing a large area with a variety of hardy annuals, or planning a mixture of hardy and half-hardy varieties, mark the sown patches with boundaries of light-coloured sand – a traditional but still effective way of seeing just where you have been! By sowing in short drills within these marked areas it is easy to tell the annuals from the weeds because they come up in rows.

Indoors, half-hardy annuals are sown ideally in a heated propagator with temperature control, and this piece of 'kit' is virtually essential when raising plants like pelargoniums (bedding geraniums) and begonias – both of which need high, constant, temperatures. Otherwise a brightly lit windowsill in a warm kitchen will work wonders – many half-hardy annuals are very undemanding once they have come up, and if not kept over-wet will grow steadily even in quite cool conditions.

Narrow 'windowsill propagators' are available which have a heated base and allow you to move pots on and off as seedlings appear – these are invaluable if you plan to do a lot of seed-raising. For all the plants in this book a 9cm (3½in) diameter pot is sufficient for the germination of an average packet of half-hardy annual seeds. If you raise half-hardy annuals remember that they will not be able to go out until after the last spring frosts. You can sow many plants later than the 'ideal' times – this book describes the optimum sowing times unless otherwise stated – and to plan for a later display of flowers with the advantage of them being easier to raise and look after a little later in the spring season.

## SOIL PREPARATION

All that annuals need to grow well is soil that has had plenty of 'organic matter' added before sowing or planting, and this is best done by digging it in thoroughly the previous autumn or in early spring. Suppliers of manure take some tracking down these days, so using home-made compost (or leaf mould) is a better option. Whatever you use, it must be dark, well-rotted, and thoroughly broken down. Organic matter is vital for improving the soil's ability to hold onto moisture at the height of summer, and also supplies some plant foods. To take proper care of feeding, scatter pelleted poultry manure over the area 2–3 weeks before sowing/planting and rake it in. This should provide ample nutrients for the rest of the summer.

## THINNING OUT

'Thinning out' or 'thinning' means allowing enough room for plants to develop fully. This is most important with hardy annuals – as young seedlings grow larger some are gradually removed to leave room for those left behind. Make sure you put your fingers on the soil when pulling plants out or there is a risk the plants you leave behind will be uprooted. Water well after thinning to settle seedlings back in. Thinning can start when plants are just 2.5cm (1in) tall and is usually finished by early summer. Autumn-sown annuals should be thinned in spring, in case some plants are lost during the winter months.

## GROWING ON

Once seedlings have been transplanted (moved) to either individual pots or cell trays, they are 'grown on'. This stage lasts until they are finally hardened off before planting out outdoors or in pots. During growing on, make sure plants do not dry out, space them out (if pot-grown) as they develop, and keep an eye out for pests and diseases. Some plants (like thunbergia, black-eyed-Susan) benefit from being potted on when their roots fill the pot.

## HARDENING OFF

Toughening plants raised indoors ready for outdoor conditions is vital if they are not to suffer a growth 'check' when you put them out. Few of us have (or have the room for) the traditional 'coldframe' which was the classic way of hardening off. These days we can make use of garden fleece, which is much easier, and just as effective. From mid-May onwards plants can be stood outside on warm days, in a sunny spot. For the first week bring them in at night, then leave them out, but covered with fleece at night. Gradually, unless frost is forecast, the fleece can be left off even at night, but replaced during frosty spells. By early June, plants will be hardened off and ready to plant.

## PLANTING

Whether you are planting in beds or containers, water the pots/trays the night before to soak the roots. Planting can be done with a trowel – or even by hand on light soils. Using your hands is certainly the best way of planting up containers and hanging baskets. Never plant the base of plants deeper than they were growing originally, firm well, and water. Keep labels with plants for future reference, and note the planting date on the label as well.

## WATERING

Lack of water causes many hardy annuals to flower and then quickly die. When the soil feels dry, enough water should be given so that it really gets down to the roots – the soil should feel moist at least 15cm (6in) down. Use a trowel and check that this is happening. Containers need much more care as they rely solely on you for their water. Choosing a compost containing water-storing crystals provides the best insurance. Do not overwater early on or roots may rot, but check them at least every other day and never allow them to dry out.

## FEEDING

By mixing slow-release fertiliser granules with the compost before planting you can take care of feeding for the whole season – you just need to water. Outdoors, bedding displays will benefit from liquid feeding every 2–4 weeks. Many hardy annuals need no extra feeding and actually thrive on poor, hungry soils.

# USING ANNUALS IN YOUR GARDEN

*With annuals the sky really is the limit. You can choose to grow just hardy or half-hardy annuals, a mixture of both, or you can be more adventurous and put them to work for you in a wide range of garden situations. Or, of course, you could just leave them to do their own thing!*

Once you have annuals in your garden you will never want to be without them. Self-seeding annuals like limnanthes and nigella will want to do their own thing and grow where they fall, while others such as lavatera and ricinus are put to much better use by carefully planning where they will grow. You can find a spot for annuals in every

garden, and sometimes they can even help you out of a tight corner! What better plants could you ask for?

*ABOVE: The delicately veined flower of agrostemma, the corncockle, an easily-grown hardy annual that is sown outdoors in spring where you want it to flower.*

*AS EDGING PLANTS these* Begonia semperflorens *are a good choice – being of even height they are good for growing in lines.*

## BEDDING SCHEMES

We see annuals used in bedding schemes almost every day of our lives, on traffic roundabouts, in public parks, and in each others gardens. The 'scheme' part of the phrase comes from the fact that many of these flashy, colourful displays are pre-planned and in many ways made-to-measure. If that is the effect you are after, then you must do your homework. The 'structure' of a basic bedding scheme is quite simple – you have tall plants in the centre of the bed, and the shortest plants around the edge. In between are plants in a range of sizes and with varying growth habits, which fill the space between the tallest and the shortest. Bedding schemes can be as simple, or as elaborate, as you like. The key points to remember are to work out which plants are going where, how many you need, and of course, whether they are suited to being grown together.

## HARDY ANNUAL SCHEMES

Creating a show using just hardy annuals is both very easy and tremendous fun. The sheer range of hardy annual varieties is enormous and it is easy to be spoilt for choice. You can go out and sow an entire bed with hardy annuals at one go, then sit back and wait for the seedlings to come up. All you need to do then is keep down annual weeds (all perennial weeds should be removed before sowing), thin out every few weeks until early summer, push in twiggy

*THIS SUMMER BEDDING SCHEME features zinnias in the centre of the bed (with variegated tradescantia creeping through) then scarlet salvias, dropping down to the pink fluffy heads of ageratum, the floss flower, below.*

supports for taller, straggly plants and enjoy the show. The best effect is from bold groups of colour, so sow in patches at least 60cm (2ft) across. Sow roughly circular areas as a fool-proof guide, although interweaving shapes can create some dramatic effects, with different plants merging as they grow into each other. Take a tip from the traditions of the past and mark out the sown areas with sand, just so you know what is where, and label each patch, or mark the varieties clearly on a sketch plan if you have one.
Using just hardy annuals means there is no need for heating early in the season, and no crisis when growing space runs short. Many hardy annuals can also be sown in autumn, usually September, to grow through the winter and then give a early performance the following spring.

## CARE-FREE HARDY ANNUALS

What could be better than a plant you only buy once, but will then always have many of? It sounds too good to be true but that is just what you get with a great many hardy annuals – the self-seeders that arrive in a packet and then spread to all their favourite spots. We have to thank the origins of many of these plants for their valuable qualities. Agrostemma, the corncockle, for example, was once a common weed of cornfields, and many other care-free annuals like it thrive on the poorest and hungriest of soils. These plants will tell you where they prefer growing by seeding themselves there, and they will need no more attention other than being pulled out when they get too dominant or invasive in areas set aside for more carefully planned activities. Calendula, centaurea, eschscholzia, papaver and tropaeolum are all good examples of care-free annuals.

## BORDER FILLERS

With the sudden loss of a favourite plant your dreams of a 'perfect' border can soon evaporate, and this is where annuals can get you out of a tight spot. Any spare patch of ground can be sown, or planted, with annuals, which will grow quickly to fill any gaps. You might even scatter seeds in amongst perennial plants and let them get on with it. Lunaria, honesty, is quite at home growing amongst spring-flowering perennial euphorbias, the purple lunaria flowers making a good contrast with the pale yellow-green euphorbias. For a touch of the tropical, ricinus, the castor oil plant, is unbeatable, with its large, exotic-looking leaves in a range of colours. Sunflowers (helianthus) are always a good bet for some instant colour when needed, and the newer dwarf varieties like 'Pacino' are easy to grow in pots for planting out as and when their bright flowers are called for to perk up flagging borders.

# ABUTILON
*Flowering maple*

ABUTILON *has a distinct 'exotic' look with its hanging, bell-like flowers that are either single or bicoloured, as seen here.*

BEING A SHRUB, *abutilon can be kept from year to year in a frost-free greenhouse and planted outdoors in mixed borders in summer.*

## FEATURES

A deciduous tender shrub that is easy to raise from seed sown in spring, with maple-like leaves and showy, hanging, bell-shaped flowers in a wide range of colours. Plants make bushy growth, and are useful in summer bedding schemes and for patio containers sited in a warm spot, but they must be protected from frost. Abutilon can be kept in a conservatory or frost-free greenhouse in winter and will flower throughout spring and summer. Plants grow to 60–90cm (2–3ft) tall. Varieties such as *Abutilon pictum* 'Thompsonii', with variegated leaves, are available from garden centres as young plants in spring; these can be potted up, grown on and then planted outdoors after the last frosts.

## CONDITIONS

**Aspect**  Grow in full sun in borders or on a south-facing patio. In southern areas plants grown against a south-facing wall in well-drained soil will often survive mild winters outdoors without protection.

**Site**  Mix plenty of rotted manure/compost into soil before planting, and use multipurpose compost in containers. Soil should be well-drained but moisture-retentive for best results.

## GROWING METHOD

**Sowing**  In February, sow in 9cm (3½in) diameter pots, cover seed with its own depth of multipurpose compost, and keep at 21°C (70°F) in light. Seedlings appear over 1–2 months so check regularly. When plants are 5cm (2in) tall, pot up into 9cm (3½in) pots and grow on. Plant out in early June after the last frosts.

**Feeding**  Apply liquid feed weekly. Mix slow-release fertiliser granules with container compost.

**Problems**  Use sprays containing pirimicarb for aphids, malathion for mealy bugs and bifenthrin for red spider mite, or, on plants growing in conservatories, use natural predators.

## FLOWERING

**Season**  Flowers appear all summer outdoors, and some may appear year-round on indoor plants and those grown in southerly, mild areas, especially near the coast.

**Cutting**  Not suitable.

**General**  Plants can be potted up before frosts and kept indoors. Increase favourites by taking cuttings in spring, rooting them on a windowsill or in a heated propagator.

---

### ABUTILON AT A GLANCE

A deciduous shrub grown as a summer bedding and container plant, with bell-like flowers. Frost hardy to −5°C (23°F).

| | | |
|---|---|---|
| JAN | / | |
| FEB | sow | |
| MAR | pot up | |
| APR | pot on | |
| MAY | harden off/plant | |
| JUN | flowering | |
| JULY | flowering | |
| AUG | flowering | |
| SEPT | flowering | |
| OCT | / | |
| NOV | / | |
| DEC | / | |

RECOMMENDED VARIETIES

Abutilon hybrids:
  'Large Flowered Mixed'
  'Mixed Colours'

# AGERATUM
## *Floss flower*

*AGERATUM FLOWERS are carried on neat-growing plants and are good for 'cooling down' other plants with bright flowers.*

*MODERN VARIETIES of ageratum for bedding produce masses of flowers which gradually rise above the leaves as they open.*

## FEATURES

Ageratum, a half-hardy annual, has fluffy long-lived flowers in blue, pink, white and bicolours such as blue-white. Use dwarf varieties for edging, as they grow up to 15cm (6in). Tall varieties are used in borders and for cutting, growing to 75cm (2½ft). Use for bedding/containers. Available as young plants.

## CONDITIONS

**Aspect**  Needs full sun and a sheltered position.

| AGERATUM AT A GLANCE | |
|---|---|
| A half-hardy annual grown for its fluffy flowers, ideal for edging, bedding, containers and cutting. Frost hardy to 0°C (32°F). | |

| | | RECOMMENDED VARIETIES |
|---|---|---|
| JAN | / | *Ageratum houstonianum:* |
| FEB | sow | **For bedding** |
| MAR | sow | 'Adriatic' |
| APR | grow on | 'Bavaria' |
| MAY | plant | 'Blue Champion' |
| JUN | flowering | 'Blue Mink' |
| JULY | flowering | 'Pink Powderpuffs' |
| AUG | flowering | 'White Blue' |
| SEPT | flowering | 'Capri' |
| OCT | / | 'White Hawaii' |
| NOV | / | **For cutting** |
| DEC | / | 'Blue Horizon' |

**Site**  Prefers well-drained soil enriched with rotted manure or compost well ahead of planting. In containers use multipurpose compost and ensure that there is good drainage.

## GROWING METHOD

**Sowing**  Sow seeds in 9cm (3½in) pots in February/March and just cover, and keep at 21°C (70°F). Seedlings appear after a week and can be moved to cell trays of multipurpose compost when two leaves are developed. Harden off and plant outside after frosts, spacing tall varieties 30–40 cm (12–16in) apart, dwarf varieties 10–15cm (4–6in) apart.

**Feeding**  Apply liquid feed fortnightly to maintain strong growth, or mix slow-release fertiliser with compost before planting up.

**Problems**  Ageratum can suffer from root rot so grow in well-drained containers on heavy clay soils, and avoid getting the compost too wet.

## FLOWERING

**Season**  Flowers appear all summer until the first frosts. Regular dead-heading, especially after heavy rain, will prolong flowering and often encourage a second 'flush' of colour.

**Cutting**  Tall varieties are suitable for cutting.

## AFTER FLOWERING

**General**  Remove plants when past their best, usually after the first sharp frosts of autumn.

# AGROSTEMMA

*Corncockle*

*SOFT PINK 'Milas' is one of the best known of the corncockle varieties. Pink and white varieties are also available.*

*GROW AGROSTEMMA in bold clumps in borders where the tall lanky, swaying plants help to give each other support.*

## FEATURES

A very easily grown hardy annual for use in cottage gardens and borders where it self-seeds year after year. Plants are tall, growing 60–90cm (2–3ft) tall, and carry pink, purple or white trumpet-like blooms. The seeds are poisonous. Commonly known as corncockle.

## CONDITIONS

**Aspect**  Grow in full sun.

---

### AGROSTEMMA AT A GLANCE

A tall hardy annual grown for its pink, purple or white flowers which are ideal for cottage borders. Frost hardy to −15°C (5°F).

| | | |
|---|---|---|
| JAN | / | |
| FEB | / | |
| MAR | sow | |
| APR | thin out | |
| MAY | flowering | |
| JUN | flowering | |
| JULY | flowering | |
| AUG | flowering | |
| SEPT | flowering | |
| OCT | sow | |
| NOV | / | |
| DEC | / | |

RECOMMENDED VARIETIES

*Agrostemma githago:*
  'Milas'
  'Ocean Pearl'
  'Purple Queen'
  'Rose of Heaven'

---

**Site**  Succeeds on well-drained and even light, sandy soils that are quite 'hungry' (it used to grow as a weed in cornfields). Excessive feeding may actually reduce the number of flowers.

## GROWING METHOD

**Sowing**  Sow outdoors from March onwards when the soil is warming up, in patches or drills 1cm (½in) deep where you want the plants to flower. Thin seedlings so they are eventually 15–30cm (6–12in) apart. Do not transplant. Can also be sown in pots in autumn, overwintered in a sheltered spot then potted up in spring for flowers in early summer.

**Feeding**  Extra feeding is unnecessary, but water occasionally but thoroughly in dry spells.

**Problems**  Agrostemma is a floppy plant and twiggy supports can be useful.

## FLOWERING

**Season**  Summer onwards, but earlier flowers are produced by autumn sowing.

**Cutting**  Short-lived as a cut flower, and rather floppy.

## AFTER FLOWERING

**General**  Dead-heading throughout summer will keep flowers coming but always leave a few to ripen and set seeds. Plants will self-sow and germinate the following spring. Alternatively, collect seedheads in paper bags and store.

# ALCEA
## *Hollyhock*

FLOWERS OF ALCEA *come in a wide range of colours and are carried along the entire length of the tall leafy stems.*

THE TALL STEMS *of hollyhocks tend to lean over as they mature, so support them at the base with short lengths of bamboo cane.*

## FEATURES

Alcea is also known as althaea, and is the familiar 'hollyhock' found in cottage borders. Flowers are single or double in a range of colours, and carried on stems which can be up to 2.5m (8ft) tall depending on variety. Tall varieties are best at the back of borders. Alcea is grown as an annual sown in spring, or as a biennial sown in summer. Spring-sown plants suffer less with rust disease. Fully hardy.

## CONDITIONS

**Aspect**    Needs full sun.
**Site**      Plants can often be found growing in cracks between paving slabs and in walls but the tallest spikes are produced by adding generous amounts of rotted manure or compost to the soil before planting. Soil must have good drainage. In windy spots stake tall varieties.

## GROWING METHOD

**Sowing**    To grow as an annual sow seed in 9cm (3½in) pots of multipurpose compost in February. Just cover the seeds and keep at 20°C (68°F). Seedlings appear in about two weeks and can be transplanted to individual 9cm (3½in) pots of compost. Grow on and plant in May after hardening off. Seeds can also be sown outdoors in April. To grow as biennials, sow seed in midsummer but germinate outdoors in a shaded spot. Plant in September.
**Feeding**   A monthly liquid feed encourages growth.
**Problems**  Rust disease spoils the look of and weakens growth and is worse in wet summers. Control is difficult but for a few plants pick off leaves and try a spray containing mancozeb.

## FLOWERING

**Season**    Early spring-sown plants grow rapidly and flower from early summer. Those planted in autumn will overwinter in the ground and flower in early summer the following season.
**Cutting**   Striking as cut flowers – take them when there are plenty of flowerbuds still to open.

## AFTER FLOWERING

**General**   Leave a few spikes to set self-sown seeds, but remove dead plants to reduce rust problems.

### ALCEA AT A GLANCE

A hardy biennial grown as an annual or biennial for its tall spikes of flowers suited to cottage gardens. Frost hardy to −15°C (5°F).

| JAN | / | RECOMMENDED VARIETIES |
|-----|------|-----------------------|
| FEB | sow | *Alcea rosea:* |
| MAR | grow on | **Single flowered** |
| APR | sow outdoors |   'Nigra' |
| MAY | plant |   'Single Mixed' |
| JUN | flowers/sow | **Double flowered** |
| JULY | flowering |   'Chater's Double Mixed' |
| AUG | flowering |   'Majorette Mixed' |
| SEPT | flowers/plant |   'Peaches 'n' Dreams' |
| OCT | / |   'Powder Puffs Mixed' |
| NOV | / |   'Summer Carnival Mixed' |
| DEC | / | |

# AMARANTHUS

*Love-lies-bleeding*

*SOME AMARANTHUS produce masses of copper-crimson leaves in summer and red flower spikes. They make good pot plants.*

*'JOSEPH'S COAT', 60cm (2ft) tall, has striking gold and crimson upper leaves, and green-yellow lower leaves marked with brown.*

## FEATURES

Amaranthus is grown for its colourful, exotic-looking foliage and its, spikey, erect or drooping tassels of blood-red, green, golden-brown, purple or multi-coloured flowers up to 45cm (18in) long. Leaves can be red, bronze, yellow, brown or green, depending on the variety grown. Size ranges from 38cm (15in) to 1.2m (4ft) tall. Use plants as pot plants, in patio containers and as dramatic centrepieces in summer bedding displays. Superb used cut for fresh or dried flower arrangements indoors.

## CONDITIONS

**Aspect**    Full sun and shelter is essential for success.
**Site**      Soil should be well-drained, with plenty of

### AMARANTHUS AT A GLANCE

A half-hardy annual grown for its leaves and flowers for bedding, containers and for drying. Frost hardy to 0°C (32°F).

| Jan | / | Recommended Varieties |
|-----|-----|-----|
| Feb | / | |
| Mar | sow | *Amaranthus caudatus:* |
| Apr | transplant | 'Green Thumb' |
| May | transplant | 'Viridis' |
| Jun | flowering | *Amaranthus cruentus:* |
| July | flowering | 'Golden Giant' |
| Aug | flowering | 'Split Personality' |
| Sept | flowering | 'Ruby Slippers' |
| Oct | flowering | *Amaranthus hybridus:* |
| Nov | / | 'Intense Purple' |
| Dec | / | *Amaranthus tricolor:* |
| | | 'Aurora Yellow' |
| | | 'Joseph's Coat' |

rotted compost or manure added. Varieties of *Amaranthus caudatus* will also succeed on thin, dry soils. Use multipurpose compost in containers and pots. In northern areas grow in 20–25cm (8–10in) diameter pots in the greenhouse or conservatory. Tall growing varieties may need staking.

## GROWING METHOD

**Sowing**    Sow seeds in March at 21°C (70°F) in 9cm (3½in) diameter pots of multipurpose compost, just covering the seed. Seeds germinate in 7–14 days or sooner, and should be transplanted into cell trays or 9cm (3½in) diameter pots of multipurpose compost. Plant outside after the last frosts in late May/early June, 30–90cm (1–3ft) apart and water.

**Feeding**   Feed weekly from early summer onwards with general-purpose liquid feed. In containers, mix slow-release fertiliser with compost before planting, and feed every two weeks with half-strength liquid feed as well.

**Problems**  Aphids can feed on the colourful leaves and build up into large colonies unless caught early. Use a spray containing permethrin.

## FLOWERING

**Season**    Foliage is colourful from early summer onwards, and is joined by flowerheads and then colourful seedheads later on.

**Cutting**   Varieties grown for their flowers can be cut and used fresh, while seedheads can be left to develop, then cut and dried for indoor use.

## AFTER FLOWERING

**General**   Remove plants when past their best.

# ANTIRRHINUM

*Snapdragon*

*OLDER VARIETIES of snapdragon like this actually have flowers that 'snap' when squeezed. This trick is not found in newer types.*

*DWARF VARIETIES reaching just 15cm (6in) are colourful for bed edges and have bushy growth without the need for pinching out.*

## FEATURES

Antirrhinums fall into three groups: tall varieties up to 1.2m (4ft) for cutting; 'intermediates' for bedding, 45cm (18in); dwarf varieties for edging/containers, 30cm (12in). Colour range is wide, and includes bicolours, and doubles. Flowers of older varieties open when squeezed at the sides, hence the name 'snapdragon'. Grow as a half-hardy annual. Available as young plants.

## CONDITIONS

**Aspect**     Must be in full sun all day.

### ANTIRRHINUM AT A GLANCE

A half-hardy annual grown for its tubular flowers, used for containers, bedding displays and cutting. Frost hardy to 0°C (32°F).

| | | RECOMMENDED VARIETIES |
|---|---|---|
| JAN | / | *Antirrhinum majus:* |
| FEB | sow | **For containers** |
| MAR | sow | 'Lipstick Silver' |
| APR | grow on | 'Magic Carpet Mixed' |
| MAY | plant | 'Tom Thumb Mixed' |
| JUN | flowering | **For bedding** |
| JULY | flowering | 'Brighton Rock Mixed' |
| AUG | flowering | 'Corona Mixed' |
| SEPT | flowering | 'Sonnet Mixed' |
| OCT | / | **For cutting** |
| NOV | / | 'Liberty Mixed' |
| DEC | / | |

**Site**     Soil must be very well-drained but have plenty of rotted compost or manure dug in before planting. In containers use multipurpose compost and ensure good, free drainage.

## GROWING METHOD

**Sowing**     Sow in February/March and barely cover the very fine seed. Use 9cm (3½in) pots of multipurpose compost and keep in light at 18°C (64°F). Seedlings appear after a week and can be transplanted to cell trays when two young leaves have developed. Plant outside after hardening off following the last frosts, 15–45cm (6–18in) apart depending on the variety. Those grown for bedding purposes should have the growing tip pinched out when 15cm (6in) tall to encourage bushy growth.

**Feeding**     Liquid feed plants in beds with a hand-held feeder fortnightly. Mix slow-release fertiliser with container compost before planting up.

**Problems**     Seedlings are prone to 'damping off' so water pots with a copper-based fungicide. Plants suffer with rust disease. Grow a 'resistant' variety such as 'Monarch Mixed' or use a spray containing penconazole at regular intervals.

## FLOWERING

**Season**     Flowers appear all summer and should be removed as they fade to keep buds coming.

**Cutting**     Tall varieties are excellent as cut spikes.

## AFTER FLOWERING

**General**     Pull plants up when they are over.

# ARCTOTIS
*African daisy*

*AFRICAN DAISIES should be pinched out when they are 12.5cm (5in) tall to encourage branching and masses of summer flowers.*

*WHEN PLANTED in groups of 3–6 plants, arctotis will form spreading clumps in sunny, south-facing borders and on banks.*

## FEATURES

African daisy is a perennial grown as a half-hardy annual for its flowers in shades of pink, red, yellow, gold, white and even blue, often with darker centre. Plants reach 45cm (18in) in height and have attractive silvery leaves. Use in bedding or as a container plant. Flowers are good for cutting.

## CONDITIONS

**Aspect** Must have full sun all day long for the flowers to stay open and give the best display, so choose a south-facing border, patio or bank. Soil must be well-drained but moisture-retentive, so work in rotted compost before planting. In containers use multipurpose compost and ensure drainage by adding a 5cm (2in) layer of gravel or polystyrene chunks.

**Site**

| ARCTOTIS AT A GLANCE | | |
|---|---|---|
| A half-hardy annual grown for its flowers, used in bedding, containers and as a cut flower. Frost hardy to 0°C (32°F). | | |

| | | RECOMMENDED VARIETIES |
|---|---|---|
| Jan | / | *Arctotis hybrida:* |
| Feb | sow |  'Harlequin' |
| Mar | sow |  'Special Hybrids Mixed' |
| Apr | transplant |  'Treasure Chest' |
| May | transplant |  'T&M Hybrids' |
| Jun | flowering | |
| July | flowering | *Arctotis hirsuta* |
| Aug | flowering | |
| Sept | flowering | *Arctotis venusta* |
| Oct | / | |
| Nov | / | |
| Dec | / | |

## GROWING METHOD

**Sowing** Sow in February/March in small pots of multipurpose compost, just covering the seed, and keep at 18°C (64°F). Seedlings appear in 2–3 weeks and are transplanted individually into 9cm (3½in) pots. Grow on, harden off at the end of May before planting after frosts, spacing plants 30–45cm (12–18in) apart.

**Feeding** Extra feeding is rarely necessary but container-grown plants benefit from liquid feed every two weeks. Avoid getting the compost too wet, especially in cooler, wet spells.

**Problems** Grows poorly on heavy, badly drained soils. Plants in containers must receive full sun.

## FLOWERING

**Season** Flowers from early summer onwards.
**Cutting** A useful but short-lived cut flower.

## AFTER FLOWERING

**General** Pot up before frosts and keep dry and frost-free over winter. Take and root cuttings in spring.

# BEGONIA
## *Begonia*

*FOR BEDDING DISPLAYS in partial shade few plants can equal the mixed varieties of* Begonia semperflorens, *seen here.*

*IN CONTAINERS begonias give a show from early summer, and you can choose dark-leaved types for specific colour schemes.*

## FEATURES

Excellent for bedding and containers, begonias have fleshy green or bronze leaves and flowers in many colours, and are grown as half-hardy annuals. 'Fibrous' rooted varieties of *Begonia semperflorens* grow up to 20cm (8in), have many small flowers and do well in shaded spots. 'Tuberous' rooted types reach 25cm (10in) tall with fewer but larger flowers up to 10cm (4in) across. Trailing varieties are also available for hanging baskets, reaching 30–60cm (1–2ft). Flowers are in mixed or single colours. A wide range of all types are available as young plants.

## CONDITIONS

**Aspect**      Will succeed best in partial shade with at least

### BEGONIA AT A GLANCE

A half-hardy annual grown for its flowers and green/bronze foliage, useful for bedding/containers. Frost hardy to 0°C (32°F).

| | | RECOMMENDED VARIETIES |
|---|---|---|
| JAN | sow 🌱 | *Begonia semperflorens:* |
| FEB | sow 🌱 | 'Ambassador Mixed' |
| MAR | transplant 🌱 | 'Cocktail Mixed' |
| APR | grow on 🌱 | 'Pink Sundae' |
| MAY | harden off 🌱 | **Tuberous varieties** |
| JUN | flowering 🌼 | 'Non-Stop Mixed' |
| JULY | flowering 🌼 | 'Non-Stop Appleblossom' |
| AUG | flowering 🌼 | 'Pin-Up' |
| SEPT | flowering 🌼 | **Trailing varieties** |
| OCT | / | 'Illumination Mixed' |
| NOV | / | 'Show Angels Mixed' |
| DEC | / | |

**Site**

some protection from direct hot sun.
Soil should be very well prepared with plenty of rotted manure or compost mixed in. Begonias produce masses of fine feeding roots. Plants do not like very heavy clay soils that stay wet for long periods, so grow in containers if necessary, using multipurpose compost when potting up in spring.

## GROWING METHOD

**Sowing**      Sow January/February. Seed is as fine as dust, so mix with a little dry silver sand and sow on the surface of 9cm (3½in) pots of seed compost based on peat or coir. Stand the pot in tepid water until the compost looks moist. Keep at 21°C (70°F) in a heated propagator in a light spot, and carefully transplant seedlings to cell trays when they have produced several tiny leaves. Seed raising is a challenge so consider growing from young plants. Plant outdoors after the last frosts in early June, 15–20cm (6–8in) apart depending on variety.

**Feeding**      Water regularly in dry spells and liquid feed bedding displays every 2–3 weeks, or mix slow-release fertiliser with compost first.

**Problems**      Overwatering causes root rot and death. Remove faded flowers, especially in wet spells.

## FLOWERING

**Season**      Flowers from early summer until frost.
**Cutting**      Not suitable as a cut flower.

## AFTER FLOWERING

**General**      Varieties that form round tubers can be potted up in autumn, dried off and then grown again the following spring.

# BELLIS
## *Daisy*

VARIETIES OF BELLIS *differ greatly. Some have small flowers with yellow centres, or the whole flower is a mass of fine petals.*

AFTER THE SPRING SHOW *is over bellis can be replanted on rockeries where it will grow as a perennial in spreading clumps.*

## FEATURES

All varieties of bellis are related to garden daisies, and are perennials grown as hardy biennials. Use in spring bedding and containers, with bulbs like tulips. Plants are spreading, 10–20cm (4–8in) high, with white, pink, red or bicoloured double or 'eyed' flowers. Petals can be tubular, or fine and needle-like. Available as young plants.

## CONDITIONS

**Aspect**  Needs a sunny, warm spot to encourage early flowers when grown for spring displays.

**Site**  Most soils are suitable, but adding well-rotted manure or compost before planting increases plant vigour and flower size. In containers use multipurpose compost and make sure the container is very free draining.

## GROWING METHOD

**Sowing**  Sow seed outdoors in May/June in fine soil in drills 1cm (½in) deep. Keep well-watered and when plants are large enough, space small clumps out in rows, 10–15cm (4–6in) apart. Alternatively, pot up into 9cm (3½in) pots. Grow on during the summer, then water, lift carefully and plant out in beds or containers in autumn, spacing 15–20cm (6–8in) apart.

**Feeding**  Liquid feed can be given every 2–3 weeks in spring when growth starts, but avoid feeding in winter, and take special care not to overwater containers or plants will rot off.

**Problems**  Bellis is trouble-free.

## FLOWERING

**Season**  Flowers appear from early spring into summer. Removal of faded flowers helps prolong flowering and reduces self-seeding.

**Cutting**  Can be used in small spring posies.

## AFTER FLOWERING

**General**  Plants are removed to make way for summer bedding and can be either discarded or replanted and left to grow as perennials.

---

### BELLIS AT A GLANCE

A perennial grown as a biennial for spring bedding displays and used with bulbs in patio containers. Frost hardy to –15ºC (5ºF).

| | | |
|---|---|---|
| JAN | / | **RECOMMENDED VARIETIES** |
| FEB | flowering | *Bellis perennis:* |
| MAR | flowering | **Small flowers** |
| APR | flowering | 'Carpet Mixed' |
| MAY | flowers/sow | 'Medici Mixed' |
| JUN | sow | 'Pomponette Mixed' |
| JULY | grow on | 'Pomponette Pink Buttons' |
| AUG | grow on | **Large flowers** |
| SEPT | grow on | 'Blush' |
| OCT | plant | 'Giant Flowered Mixed' |
| NOV | / | 'Goliath Mixed' |
| DEC | / | 'Habanera Mixed' |

# BRACHYSCOME
*Swan river daisy*

*SWAN RIVER DAISIES produce mounds of small, daisy-like flowers in profusion throughout the summer months.*

*FOR MIXED SHADES and 'eyes' of different colours choose an up-to-date variety of* Brachyscome iberidifolia *such as 'Bravo Mixed'.*

## FEATURES

Brachyscome is covered in mounds of daisy flowers, and is good in beds and in hanging baskets and patio containers. It makes an effective edging plant where it can develop unhindered without being crowded out by more vigorous plants. Leaves are light green and feathery with a delicate appearance. Plants grow 23cm (9in) tall with a similar spread. Choose single colours or mixtures. Brachyscome can be planted in May before the last frosts, and will tolerate short dry spells. A half-hardy annual, also seen as 'brachycome'.

## CONDITIONS

**Aspect**    Choose a south-facing position in full sun.

### BRACHYSCOME AT A GLANCE

A half-hardy annual grown for its daisy-like flowers, useful for bedding, baskets and containers. Frost hardy to 0°C (32°F)

| | | |
|---|---|---|
| JAN | / | |
| FEB | / | |
| MAR | sow | |
| APR | sow/transplant | |
| MAY | plant outdoors | |
| JUN | flowering | |
| JULY | flowering | |
| AUG | flowering | |
| SEPT | flowering | |
| OCT | / | |
| NOV | / | |
| DEC | / | |

RECOMMENDED VARIETIES

*Brachyscome iberidifolia:*
  'Blue Star'
  'Bravo Mixed'
  'Mixed'
  'Purple Splendour'
  'White Splendour'

**Site**    Choose a warm, sheltered spot away from wind. Brachyscome likes rich, well-drained soil, with plenty of rotted compost or manure added. Use multipurpose potting compost in containers.

## GROWING METHOD

**Sowing**    Sow in March and April in 9cm (3½in) diameter pots, just covering the seeds, and germinate at 18°C (64°F). Seedlings emerge within three weeks. Transplant into cell trays of multipurpose compost, and plant out in beds 23–30cm (9–12in) apart.

**Feeding**    Liquid feed each week outdoors. Add slow-release fertiliser granules to container compost, and also liquid feed every two weeks in summer. Avoid overwatering, especially in dull, wet spells or plants may rot off.

**Problems**    Support floppy plants with small twigs. Avoid planting among large, vigorous container plants that will swamp low growers and cast them in shade at the height of summer. Control slugs with pellets or set slug traps in bedding displays.

## FLOWERING

**Season**    Flowers appear all summer and are faintly scented – this is best appreciated by growing them at nose height in hanging baskets, flower bags and windowboxes.

**Cutting**    Not suitable.

## AFTER FLOWERING

**General**    Remove when flowers are over and add to the compost heap or bin.

# BRASSICA
*Ornamental cabbage and kale*

*ORNAMENTAL KALES help pack a punch in the garden during autumn with their bright leaves that deepen in colour when the temperature falls below 10°C (50°F). Plants grown in containers should be kept in a sheltered spot during spells of severe winter weather.*

## FEATURES

Ornamental cabbages and kales are grown for colourful autumn and winter foliage, growing 30–45cm (12–18in) tall and wide. Use for bedding or large pots. Leaf colour is pink, rose or white and improves with temperatures below 10°C (50°F). Damage is caused by severe frost. Available as young plants.

## CONDITIONS

**Aspect**    Needs full sun to develop good colour.

### BRASSICA AT A GLANCE

A hardy annual grown for its brightly coloured leaves which last from autumn until spring. Frost hardy to –15°C (5°F).

| | | |
|---|---|---|
| JAN | leaves | |
| FEB | leaves | |
| MAR | leaves | |
| APR | leaves | |
| MAY | leaves | |
| JUN | sow | |
| JULY | sow | |
| AUG | grow-on | |
| SEPT | plant | |
| OCT | leaves | |
| NOV | leaves | |
| DEC | leaves | |

RECOMMENDED VARIETIES

**Cabbages**
 'Delight Mixed'
 'Northern Lights'
 'Ornamental Mixed'
 'Tokyo Mixed'

**Kales**
 'Nagoya Mixed'
 'Red & White Peacock'
 'Red Chidori'

**Site**    Enrich soil with rotted compost or manure ahead of planting. Adding lime will improve results on acid soils. Avoid spots exposed to driving winter winds. Plant up containers using multipurpose compost making sure pots and tubs are free draining.

## GROWING METHOD

**Sowing**    Seed is sown in June/July in 9cm (3½in) pots of multipurpose compost and kept out of the sun. Large seedlings appear after a week and are transplanted to individual 9cm (3½in) pots. Grow these on outdoors, watering frequently, and then plant out in beds or in containers in early autumn where the display is required.

**Feeding**    Give a high-potash liquid feed fortnightly throughout the summer months. Tomato food is suitable and encourages leaf colour.

**Problems**    Cabbage caterpillars will also attack ornamental varieties and kales. Pick off by hand or use a spray containing permethrin.

## FLOWERING

**Season**    Plants are at their best in autumn and early winter. Any surviving the winter will produce tall clusters of yellow flowers in spring.

**Cutting**    Whole heads makes a striking, unusual element in winter flower arrangements.

## AFTER FLOWERING

**General**    Remove in spring or if killed by frosts.

# BROWALLIA

*Bush violet*

*BROWALLIA FLOWERS have an almost crystalline texture when lit by the sun. They appear in masses on rounded plants, and at the height of summer can almost completely hide the leaves. Seen here are the varieties 'Blue Troll' and 'White Troll'.*

## FEATURES

Browallia takes its common name from its violet-blue flowers which have a pale 'eye'. White flowered varieties and mixtures are available. Plants grow up to 30cm (12in) and are suitable for containers and baskets, and in warmer areas, bedding. Varieties of *Browallia speciosa* are grown as half-hardy annuals and can also be used as indoor pot plants.

## CONDITIONS

**Aspect**    Needs a warm, sheltered spot in sun.

### BROWALLIA AT A GLANCE

A half-hardy annual grown for its blue, white or pink flowers, useful for bedding/container planting. Frost hardy to 0ºC (32ºF).

| | | | |
|---|---|---|---|
| JAN | / | RECOMMENDED VARIETIES | |
| FEB | sow | *Browallia speciosa:* | |
| MAR | sow | **Blue flowers** | |
| APR | grow on | 'Blue Troll' | |
| MAY | plant | 'Blue Bells' | |
| JUN | flowering | 'Starlight Blue' | |
| JULY | flowering | | |
| AUG | flowering | **White flowers** | |
| SEPT | flowering | 'White Troll' | |
| OCT | / | | |
| NOV | / | **Blue/pink/white flowers** | |
| DEC | / | 'Jingle Bells' | |

**Site**    Browallia does not tolerate poor drainage, and on heavy soils should only be grown as a container plant, using multipurpose compost. Otherwise, mix in well-rotted compost or manure several weeks before planting out.

## GROWING METHOD

**Sowing**    For summer bedding sow the seed on the surface of 9cm (3½in) pots of multipurpose compost in February/March. Keep at 18ºC (64ºF) and do not let the surface dry out. Seedlings appear in 2–3 weeks and should be transplanted to individual cell trays or 7.5cm (3in) pots. Harden off at the end of May and plant in early June. For flowering pot plants seed can be sown in the same way until June.

**Feeding**    Give plants a liquid feed fortnightly or, in containers and windowboxes, mix slow-release fertiliser with the compost first.

**Problems**    Aphids sometimes attack the soft leaves so use a spray containing permethrin if they appear.

## FLOWERING

**Season**    Flowers appear from early summer onwards and continue until the first frosts. Take off faded flowers regularly to encourage buds.

**Cutting**    Not suitable as a cut flower.

## AFTER FLOWERING

**General**    Plants die when frosts arrive. Pot plants indoors can be kept going indefinitely.

# CALCEOLARIA

*Slipper flower*

*THE HOT COLOURS OF THE 'SUNSET' strain of calceolaria excel outdoors and combine well with marigolds.*

## FEATURES

Only a few varieties of calceolaria are suitable for outdoors; these are different to the indoor pot type. By nature shrubs, they are grown from seed each year as hardy annuals and are useful for bedding and containers. None grow more than 40cm (16in) tall and wide.

## CONDITIONS

**Aspect**      Needs full sun or part shade.

### CALCEOLARIA AT A GLANCE

A half-hardy annual, calceolaria is used for bedding and containers, with bright flowers. Frost hardy to 0°C (32°F).

| | | |
|---|---|---|
| JAN | sow | |
| FEB | sow | |
| MAR | transplant | |
| APR | grow on | |
| MAY | harden off | |
| JUN | flowering | |
| JULY | flowering | |
| AUG | flowering | |
| SEPT | flowering | |
| OCT | / | |
| NOV | / | |
| DEC | / | |

RECOMMENDED VARIETIES

**Calceolaria hybrids:**
'Little Sweeties Mixed'
'Midas'
'Sunshine'
'Sunset Mixed'

**Site**        Slipper flowers thrive in moist soil where their roots stay as cool as possible. Mix in well-rotted compost or manure before planting and use a peat- or coir-based multipurpose compost for filling containers.

## GROWING METHOD

**Sowing**      The fine seed can be sown on the surface of peat- or coir-based multipurpose compost in a 9cm (3½in) pot, January–March, at a temperature of 18°C (64°F). Keep in a bright place. Seedlings appear in 2–3 weeks and can be transplanted to cell trays, then hardened off and planted after frosts, 15–30cm (6–12in) apart, or used with other plants in containers.

**Feeding**     Liquid feed every 3–4 weeks or mix slow-release fertiliser with compost before planting.

**Problems**    Slugs will eat the leaves of young plants in wet spells during early summer. Protect plants with a barrier of grit or eggshell or scatter slug pellets sparingly around plants.

## FLOWERING

**Season**      Plants will flower from early summer until frosts. Take off dead flowers weekly.

**Cutting**     A few stems can be taken but avoid damaging the overall shape and appearance of the plant.

## AFTER FLOWERING

**General**     Remove plants in autumn when finished.

# CALENDULA
## *Pot marigold*

MIXED VARIETIES *of calendula offer a wide colour range, most commonly shades of orange and yellow as seen here.*

CALENDULA *is a bushy plant producing masses of summer flowers – the edible petals can be scattered on summer salads.*

## FEATURES

Also known as English marigold, calendula is a fast-growing, hardy annual with daisy-type flowers in shades of yellow, orange, red, pinkish and even green. Flowers can be fully double while others have a distinct darker 'eye'. The edible petals can be used in salads. Perfect for a cottage garden bed or border, and very easy to grow, the large curled seeds are sown straight into the soil outdoors. Plant size ranges from 30–70cm (12–28in) tall and wide.

## CONDITIONS

**Aspect**  Needs full sun to succeed.
**Site**  Does well even in poor soil, which can actually increase the number of flowers. Add rotted organic matter to the soil ahead of planting

### CALENDULA AT A GLANCE

A hardy annual for growing in beds and borders and a useful cut flower in many shades. Frost hardy to −15ºC (5ºF).

| | | RECOMMENDED VARIETIES |
|---|---|---|
| JAN | / | *Calendula officinalis:* |
| FEB | / | 'Art Shades Mixed' |
| MAR | sow | 'Fiesta Gitana Mixed' |
| APR | sow | 'Greenheart Orange' |
| MAY | thin out | 'Kablouna Lemon Cream' |
| JUN | flowering | 'Kablouna Mixed' |
| JULY | flowering | 'Orange King' |
| AUG | flowers/sow | 'Pacific Beauty' |
| SEPT | flowers/sow | 'Pink Surprise' |
| OCT | / | 'Princess Mixed' |
| NOV | / | 'Radio' |
| DEC | / | 'Touch of Red Mixed' |

time to improve results. Calendula does not do well on heavy, badly drained soils, so grow in containers under these conditions.

## GROWING METHOD

**Sowing**  March to May or August/September are the sowing periods. Sow the large seeds direct into finely raked moist soil where you want plants to flower, in drills 1cm (½in) deep, and cover. Thin out as seedlings grow so that plants are eventually spaced 25–30cm (10–12in) apart. Autumn-sown plants flower earlier the following year. If flowers for cutting are required sow seed thinly in long rows.
**Feeding**  Liquid feed once a month to encourage larger blooms. Use a feed high in potash to encourage flowers rather than leafy growth – tomato fertilisers are a good choice.
**Problems**  The leaves are prone to attack by aphids causing twisting and damage. Use a spray containing permethrin, but avoid eating flowers. Powdery mildew can affect leaves in late summer but is not worth treating – pick off the worst affected leaves and compost them.

## FLOWERING

**Season**  Flowers appear in late spring on plants sown the previous autumn, and from early summer on spring-sown plants. Removal of faded blooms will keep up a succession of flowers.
**Cutting**  Good as a cut flower – cutting helps to keep flowers coming. Cut when flowers are well formed but before petals open out too far.

## AFTER FLOWERING

**General**  Pull up after flowering. Will self-seed if a few heads are left to ripen fully and shed seeds.

# CALLISTEPHUS
*China aster*

*CHINA ASTERS with their large, showy and often double flowers can be used as summer bedding plants for massed displays.*

*AS A CUT FLOWER callistephus is unrivalled for producing long-lasting blooms in late summer when other flowers are past their best.*

## FEATURES

China asters are half-hardy annuals and are not to be confused with the perennial asters or Michaelmas daisies. Grow as bedding, as cut flowers, and in large pots. Flowers come in a wide range from narrow, quill-like petals to bicolours, and also single shades. Size ranges from 20–90cm (8–36in) tall, depending on the variety. Available as young plants.

## CONDITIONS

**Aspect**      Must have a warm spot in full sun all day.

### CALLISTEPHUS AT A GLANCE

A half-hardy annual grown for its flowers, used in bedding, containers and as a cut flower. Frost hardy to 0°C (32°F).

| | | |
|---|---|---|
| JAN | / | |
| FEB | / | |
| MAR | sow | |
| APR | sow | |
| MAY | plant | |
| JUN | flowering | |
| JULY | flowering | |
| AUG | flowering | |
| SEPT | flowering | |
| OCT | flowering | |
| NOV | / | |
| DEC | / | |

RECOMMENDED VARIETIES

*Callistephus chinensis:*
  'Apricot Giant'
  'Dwarf Comet Mixed'
  'Matsumoto Mixed'
  'Moraketa'
  'Milady Mixed'
  'Ostrich Plume Mixed'
  'Red Ribbon'
  'Teisa Stars Mixed'

**Site**      Plants need well-drained soil with added organic matter such as rotted manure or compost dug in before planting. If grown in containers use multipurpose compost with slow-release fertiliser granules mixed in.

## GROWING METHOD

**Sowing**      Sow in March/April in 9cm (3½in) pots of compost and keep at 16°C (61°F). Seedlings appear after a week and can be transplanted to cell trays and grown on. Plant in late May, plants are not damaged by the last frosts. Seed can also be sown direct into the ground in late April and May. Plant 20–60cm (8–24in) apart.

**Feeding**      Water regularly and give plants in containers a general liquid feed every two weeks. In beds feed when you water with a hand-held feeder.

**Problems**      Aphids cause the leaves to distort which can affect flowering. Use a spray containing dimethoate. If plants suddenly collapse and die they are suffering from aster wilt and should be removed with the soil around their roots and put in the dustbin. Avoid growing asters in that spot and try 'resistant' varieties.

## FLOWERING

**Season**      Early summer to early autumn.
**Cutting**      An excellent and long-lasting cut flower.

## AFTER FLOWERING

**General**      Remove plants after flowering and compost any that do not show signs of wilt disease.

# CAMPANULA
## *Canterbury bells*

THE BELL-LIKE *flowers of* Campanula medium *give it its common name of Canterbury bells. It is seen here growing with ageratum.*

WHEN CANTERBURY BELLS *display this characteristic 'saucer' behind the cup-shaped bloom, they simply ooze charm.*

## FEATURES

Canterbury bells are best in massed plantings in mixed borders and are good for cutting. Dwarf varieties can be used for bedding and in containers. The large, bell-like single or double flowers are blue, pink, mauve or white, on stems 60–90cm (2–3ft) high, rising from large clumps. Usually grown as a hardy biennial, the dwarf variety 'Chelsea Pink' is grown as an annual, flowering three months after sowing in February. Stake tall plants.

## CONDITIONS

**Aspect**  Grow in an open spot in full sun.

### CAMPANULA AT A GLANCE

A hardy biennial grown for bedding and for the tall flower spikes that are ideal for cutting. Frost hardy to –15°C (5°F).

| | | |
|---|---|---|
| JAN | / | RECOMMENDED VARIETIES |
| FEB | / | |
| MAR | / | *Campanula medium:* |
| APR | sow | **Tall varieties** |
| MAY | sow | 'Calycanthema Mixed' |
| JUN | flowers/sow | 'Cup and Saucer Mixed' |
| JULY | flowering | 'Rosea' |
| AUG | flowering | 'Single Mixed' |
| SEPT | flowering | |
| OCT | plant | **Shorter/dwarf varieties** |
| NOV | / | 'Bella Series' |
| DEC | / | 'Bells of Holland' |
| | | 'Chelsea Pink' |
| | | 'Russian Pink' |

**Site**  Plenty of well-rotted manure or compost dug into the soil produces strong growth. Requires good drainage but the soil should retain moisture and not dry out completely. In containers use multipurpose compost.

## GROWING METHOD

**Sowing**  Sow the fine seed from April–June outdoors, or in small pots of multipurpose compost. Just cover the seed. Either transplant seedlings to 30cm (12in) apart or pot up individually into 9cm (3½in) pots. Grow on through the summer and plant during autumn in groups of 3–5, spacing plants 30cm (12in) apart. Flowers will appear the following summer.

**Feeding**  Give a monthly liquid feed, starting a few weeks after transplanting or potting up and make sure potted plants do not dry out. Scatter a general granular fertiliser over beds in spring to keep growth strong and encourage flowers.

**Problems**  Slugs will eat the crowns of plants in early summer, especially after rain, so scatter slug pellets or use a physical barrier like grit.

## FLOWERING

**Season**  Flower spikes appear from early summer onwards. A second 'flush' of flowers is possible if all stems are cut to the ground when faded.

**Cutting**  Good cut flower so grow extra plants of a tall variety in rows just for cutting.

## AFTER FLOWERING

**General**  Remove plants after the flowering season and add them to the compost heap or bin.

# CATHARANTHUS
## *Madagascar periwinkle*

*THE FAMILIAR FLOWERS of Catharanthus roseus look similar to those of its close relative the hardy vinca.*

*FOR BEDDING DISPLAYS catharanthus is available in mixed colours which often contain flowers with darker 'eyes' as seen here.*

## FEATURES

Varieties of *Catharanthus roseus* have pink/rose, mauve or white flowers, often with a deeper centre. Plants are spreading, growing to 25–40cm (10–16in), and suitable for massed bedding displays or pots indoors. Grow as a half-hardy annual.

## CONDITIONS

**Aspect**    Needs full sun to succeed outdoors.

### CATHARANTHUS AT A GLANCE

A half-hardy annual grown for its bright flowers and ideal for use in containers on a warm sunny patio. Frost hardy to 0°C (32°F).

| | | RECOMMENDED VARIETIES |
|---|---|---|
| JAN | / | *Catharanthus roseus:* |
| FEB | / | 'Apricot Delight' |
| MAR | sow | 'Pacifica Red' |
| APR | transplant | 'Peppermint Cooler' |
| MAY | harden off/plant | 'Pretty In... Mixed' |
| JUN | flowering | 'Tropicana Mixed' |
| JULY | flowering | 'Terrace Vermillion' |
| AUG | flowering | |
| SEPT | flowering | |
| OCT | / | |
| NOV | / | |
| DEC | / | |

**Site**    Needs good drainage but enrich the soil with well-rotted manure or compost before planting. For containers use multipurpose compost with extra slow-release fertiliser mixed in before planting up.

## GROWING METHOD

**Sowing**    Sow seed in March/April in 9cm (3½in) pots of multipurpose compost and lightly cover. Keep at 18°C (64°F) in a light spot and transplant seedlings when they are 2.5cm (1in) tall, into cell trays. Keep in a warm greenhouse or warm spot indoors and do not get the compost too wet. Harden off in late May and plant 20–30cm (8–12in) apart in their final positions or use in containers.

**Feeding**    In bedding displays, apply a liquid plant food monthly to keep plants growing vigorously throughout the summer months.

**Problems**    Overwatering and wet soil/compost can lead to rotting. If red spider mite attacks the leaves use a spray containing bifenthrin.

## FLOWERING

**Season**    Flowers appear throughout the summer.
**Cutting**    Not suitable for cutting.

## AFTER FLOWERING

**General**    Remove plants after the first autumn frosts and use for composting.

# CELOSIA
## *Prince of Wales' feathers*

*THE FEATHERY FLOWERS of celosia are made up of masses of smaller flowers, and have a distinctive, plume-like shape.*

*THE BRILLIANT PLUMES of cockscomb always look best in patio pots and containers when planted together in groups of 4–6 plants.*

## FEATURES

Also known as Prince of Wales' feathers, celosia or cockscomb has plume-like or crested flowers (shown left) ranging in colour from deep crimson to scarlet, orange and yellow. Tall forms grow to 75cm (30in), the dwarf forms to 25–30cm (10–12in). Grow it as a half-hardy annual and use in bedding or as a striking plant for containers. Good for cutting.

## CONDITIONS

**Aspect**　　Must have a sunny, warm spot to do well.

### CELOSIA AT A GLANCE

A half-hardy annual grown for its feathery, plume-like flower-heads in a range of colours. Frost hardy to 0°C (32°F).

| | | |
|---|---|---|
| JAN | / | **RECOMMENDED VARIETIES** |
| FEB | sow | **Plumed** |
| MAR | sow | *Celosia argentea:* |
| APR | pot on | 'Kimono Mixed' |
| MAY | harden off/plant | 'Dwarf Geisha' |
| JUN | flowering | 'Century Mixed' |
| JULY | flowering | 'New Look' |
| AUG | flowering | *Celosia spicata:* |
| SEPT | flowering | 'Flamingo Feather' |
| OCT | / | **Crested** |
| NOV | / | *Celosia cristata:* |
| DEC | / | 'Jewel Box Mixed' |

**Site**　　Needs well-drained soil that has been enriched with well-rotted manure or compost. Good soil preparation is essential to ensure strong plants and large flowerheads. Plant up containers using multipurpose compost

## GROWING METHOD

**Sowing**　　Celosias dislike having their roots disturbed so sow 2–3 seeds per cell in a multi-cell tray using multipurpose compost, in February/March. Keep at 18°C (64°F) and when the seedlings appear after 2–3 weeks, remove all but the strongest. Carefully pot the young plants on into 9cm (3½in) pots, then harden off for two weeks before planting after the last frosts. Plant without damaging the roots, 15–30cm (6–12in) apart, and water.

**Feeding**　　Feed bedding monthly with liquid feed. Mix slow-release fertiliser with the compost before planting up containers.

**Problems**　　Wet, cold soil/compost can cause rotting of the roots, so avoid heavy soils and grow in pots.

## FLOWERING

**Season**　　Flowers appear throughout summer.

**Cutting**　　May be used as a cut flower for unusual indoor decoration. Cut some plumes and hang them upside down in a dry, airy place for later use in dried flower arrangements.

## AFTER FLOWERING

**General**　　Remove plants after the first frosts of autumn.

# CENTAUREA

## *Cornflower*

*CORNFLOWERS should have pale, fading flowers removed regularly. For indoor use cut the stems when the buds are still closed.*

*GROWN IN GROUPS like this, cornflowers will support each other quite naturally. In windy spots push twigs in between plants.*

## FEATURES

Cornflower, *Centaurea cyanus* is, one of the easiest hardy annuals to grow and can be used in bedding, containers and for cut flowers. Other than blue, there are mixtures available and single colours such as the 'Florence' types in red, pink and white, reaching 35cm (14in) tall. Taller varieties like 'Blue Diadem' are best for cutting. Regular removal of dead flowers is essential to prolong flowering and to stop plants from becoming shabby.

### CENTAUREA AT A GLANCE

A hardy annual grown for its 'cottage garden' type flowers in various colours, useful for cutting. Frost hardy to –15°C (5°F).

| | | |
|---|---|---|
| JAN | / | |
| FEB | / | |
| MAR | sow | |
| APR | thin out | |
| MAY | flowering | |
| JUN | flowering | |
| JULY | flowering | |
| AUG | flowering | |
| SEPT | flowers/sow | |
| OCT | / | |
| NOV | / | |
| DEC | / | |

RECOMMENDED VARIETIES

*Centaurea cyanus:*
**Short varieties**
  'Florence Blue'
  'Florence Mixed'
  'Florence Pink'
  'Florence Red'
  'Florence White'
  'Midget Mixed'
**Tall varieties**
  'Blue Diadem'
  'Black Ball'

## CONDITIONS

**Aspect**    Needs full sun all day.
**Site**    Must have very well-drained soil, but no special soil preparation is necessary. Staking is necessary when grown in windy situations, but the plants are self-supporting when they are planted in groups. For container growing use multipurpose compost.

## GROWING METHOD

**Sowing**    Sow seed in spring where plants are to flower in short rows 1cm (½in) deep and about 30cm (12in) apart. Thin out so plants are finally 7.5–15cm (3–6in) apart. This can also be done in late September for stronger plants and earlier flowers, but leave thinning out until the following spring. Can also be sown in pots and transplanted to cell trays for plants to use in patio containers.
**Feeding**    Extra feeding is usually unnecessary.
**Problems**    White mildew affects leaves but is not serious.

## FLOWERING

**Season**    Summer until early autumn.
**Cutting**    Cut before the petals open out too far.

## AFTER FLOWERING

**General**    Remove plants once flowering is finished. Plants self-seed if they are left in the ground.

# CHEIRANTHUS
## *Wallflower*

*THE INTENSE COLOURS of wallflowers are only matched by their strong, lingering scent which is best on warm, still days.*

*'IVORY WHITE' is a useful single-coloured variety of* Cheiranthus cheiri *for bedding schemes which are colour-themed.*

## FEATURES

Wallflowers have fragrant flowers of yellow, brown, cream, red and orange and are grown for their sweet spring scent. These hardy biennials grow between 20–45cm (8–18in) depending on variety, and are available as mixed or single colours. Plants are used for bedding but may also be used in patio containers, where they can be moved near doors and windows when in bloom. Ready-grown plants can be bought in early autumn.

### CHEIRANTHUS AT A GLANCE

With its bright flowers and strong scent, this biennial is useful for spring bedding and for containers. Frost hardy to –15°C (5°F).

| | | |
|---|---|---|
| JAN | / | |
| FEB | flowering | ✿ |
| MAR | flowering | ✿ |
| APR | flowering | ✿ |
| MAY | sow | ✿ |
| JUN | sow | ✿ |
| JULY | thin out | ✿ |
| AUG | grow on | ✿ |
| SEPT | grow on | ✿ |
| OCT | plant | ✿ |
| NOV | / | |
| DEC | / | |

RECOMMENDED VARIETIES

*Cheiranthus cheiri:*

**Tall**
  'Blood Red'
  'Cloth of Gold'
  'Harlequin'

**Medium**
  'My Fair Lady Mixed'
  'Vulcan Improved'

**Dwarf**
  'Prince Mixed'
  'Tom Thumb Mixed'

## CONDITIONS

**Aspect** Grow in full sun for the best scent.
**Site** Must have very well-drained soil. Add lime before planting to reduce the effect of clubroot disease. Use multipurpose compost in containers and windowboxes. Avoid spots exposed to winter winds and move containers to shelter during severe winter weather.

## GROWING METHOD

**Sowing** Sow May/June outdoors in rows 30cm (12in) apart and 1cm (½in) deep. As plants grow, thin them to 30cm (12in) apart, and pinch when 7.5cm (3in) tall to make growth bushy. Can also be sown in pots and transplanted into 9cm (3½in) pots. Plant in October in beds or containers. When lifting plants keep as much soil on the roots as possible.
**Feeding** Give a liquid feed monthly during summer.
**Problems** Avoid growing in soil known to be infected with clubroot disease, or raise plants in pots using multipurpose compost.

## FLOWERING

**Season** Late winter through to spring.
**Cutting** Cut stems last well in water.

## AFTER FLOWERING

**General** Remove plants in late spring after flowering.

# CLEOME
*Spider flower*

*SPIDER FLOWERS are available as single colours or mixed. The popular 'Colour Fountains Mixed' is seen here in a summer border.*

*THE EXOTIC FEEL that cleome adds to the garden can be used to best effect on a warm patio where their scent lingers in still air.*

## FEATURES

The spider-like flowers of *Cleome spinosa*, in pink, white or rose, have narrow petals with long stamens. They appear all summer up and down the length of the stem. These large half-hardy annuals grow to 1.5m (5ft) tall with a single stem, and with lobed leaves. Plant at the back of borders or use them as central 'dot' plants in large tubs for an 'exotic' feel. Look out for the thorny stems and pungent leaves.

## CONDITIONS

**Aspect**    Needs full sun and a sheltered position to achieve maximum height during the summer.

### CLEOME AT A GLANCE

A half-hardy annual grown for its exotic flowers and ideal as a centrepiece for bedding/containers. Frost hardy to 0°C (32°F).

| | | RECOMMENDED VARIETIES |
|---|---|---|
| JAN | / | *Cleome spinosa:* |
| FEB | sow | **Mixed colours** |
| MAR | sow | 'Colour Fountain Mixed' |
| APR | grow on | |
| MAY | harden off/plant | **Single colours** |
| JUN | flowering | 'Cherry Queen' |
| JULY | flowering | 'Helen Campbell' |
| AUG | flowering | 'Pink Queen' |
| SEPT | flowering | 'Violet Queen' |
| OCT | / | |
| NOV | / | |
| DEC | / | |

**Site**    Needs good drainage but tolerates a wide range of soils. For best results improve soil by digging in rotted manure or compost, and use multipurpose compost with slow-release fertiliser added when planting containers. Stems are generally strong enough that they can be grow without extra support.

## GROWING METHOD

**Sowing**    Sow seeds in 9cm (3½in) pots of multipurpose compost in February/March and keep at 18°C (64°F). Seedlings appear after two weeks and are transplanted to 9cm (3½in) pots, grown on in a warm greenhouse or conservatory. Pot on into 12.5cm (5in) pots in early May, and harden off before planting after the last frosts.

**Feeding**    Feed plants in beds fortnightly with liquid feed from a hand-held applicator. Don't allow the compost in containers to become over-wet.

**Problems**    Aphids attack young plants and cause twisted growth. Check under the leaves regularly and use a spray with permethrin if necessary, making sure the spray gets under the leaves.

## FLOWERING

**Season**    The long flowering period extends throughout summer and well into mild autumns. The long thin seed pods give it a real 'spidery' look.

**Cutting**    Useful as a cut flower, but watch the spines.

## AFTER FLOWERING

**General**    Remove plants after flowering, but wear gloves for protection as the stems are spiny.

# CONSOLIDA
## *Larkspur*

*LARKSPUR IS DOUBLY useful as a cut flower because the spikes can be dried and used for dried flower arrangements.*

*FINELY DIVIDED LEAVES are characteristic of* Consolida *ajacis, while flowers can be single, as here, or double, in various colours.*

## FEATURES

*Consolida ajacis*, larkspur, is related to delphinium but is not as tall and is grown as a hardy annual. Ideal for a 'cottage garden' border, larkspur grows up to 90cm (3ft) tall and has spikes of pink, white, red, blue and violet single or double flowers, with finely cut leaves. Good for cutting. Seeds are poisonous.

## CONDITIONS

**Aspect**    Grow in a sunny, open spot.

### CONSOLIDA AT A GLANCE

A hardy annual grown for its spikes of bright flowers which are useful for borders and cutting. Frost hardy to −15°C (5°F).

| | | RECOMMENDED VARIETIES |
|---|---|---|
| JAN | / | *Consolida ajacis:* |
| FEB | / | **Tall, for cutting** |
| MAR | sow | 'Earl Grey' |
| APR | thin out | 'Frosted Skies' |
| MAY | thin/flowers | 'Giant Imperial Mixed' |
| JUN | flowering | 'Hyacinth Flowered |
| JULY | flowering | Mixed' |
| AUG | flowering | **Short, for bedding** |
| SEPT | flowers/sow | 'Dwarf Hyacinth |
| OCT | / | Flowered Mixed' |
| NOV | / | 'Dwarf Rocket Mixed' |
| DEC | / | |

## Site

Soil can be enriched with manure or compost well ahead of planting, but it must be well-drained. Plants will also grow well on thin and hungry soils. Plants should support each other as they grow and not need artificial support. Use taller varieties at the back of borders.

## GROWING METHOD

**Sowing**    Sow direct where the plants are to grow for best results, in short rows 1cm (½in) deep, in either March or September. Expect seedlings to appear in 2–3 weeks. Thin plants out as they grow so they are eventually 7.5–15cm (3–6in) apart depending on the variety.

**Feeding**    Extra feeding is not necessary.

**Problems**    Slugs eat young seedlings so scatter slug pellets around plants or protect them with a 5cm (2in) wide barrier of sharp grit.

## FLOWERING

**Season**    Flowers appear from spring onwards on autumn-sown plants, June onwards from spring sowings. Removing faded flower spikes will encourage more flowers.

**Cutting**    An excellent cut flower. Cut long stems and scald ends before soaking in cool water.

## AFTER FLOWERING

**General**    Leave a few plants to die down naturally and self-seed into the soil, otherwise pull up when finished and use for composting.

# COREOPSIS
## *Tickseed*

'EARLY SUNRISE' *is a semi-double variety of coreopsis usually treated as an annual, growing 45cm (18in) tall and good for cutting.*

COREOPSIS CAN FORM *very large clumps. It gets its common name 'tickseed' from seeds which look like small bugs.*

## FEATURES

Coreopsis make good garden plants with single and double flowers in yellow, red and mahogany tones, growing 25–90cm (10–36in) tall depending on the variety. Some bedding varieties are perennials but are best grown as hardy or half-hardy annuals from a spring sowing. Dwarf varieties are used in patio pots.

## CONDITIONS

**Aspect**    For best results grow in full sun.
**Site**    Tolerates poor soil, but soil which has been enriched with rotted manure/compost ahead of planting time will give stronger plants. In containers use multipurpose compost. Taller varieties should not need support if planted in groups so plants support each other.

## GROWING METHOD

**Sowing**    Sow seed February/March in 9cm (3½in) pots of multipurpose compost, just cover, and keep at 16°C (61°F). Transplant into cell trays, harden off for two weeks in late May and plant out after the last frosts. Seed can also be sown straight outdoors in May/June but expect later flowers continuing into the autumn.

**Feeding**    Should not need extra feeding if soil is well prepared. Add slow-release fertiliser to compost when planting up containers.

**Problems**    Slugs and snails will eat seedlings in spring during wet spells so protect with slug pellets.

## FLOWERING

**Season**    The flowering period lasts throughout summer, especially if spent flowers are regularly removed from the plants.

**Cutting**    Tall varieties can be used as cut flowers. Pick when flowers have opened fully but the petals are still fresh looking.

## AFTER FLOWERING

**General**    Perennial varieties such as 'Mayfield Giant' and 'Sunrise' can be lifted in autumn and planted in permanent border positions.

### COREOPSIS AT A GLANCE

A perennial grown as both as a hardy or half-hardy annual for its yellow to mahogany flowers. Frost hardy to –15°C (5°F).

| | | |
|---|---|---|
| JAN | / | |
| FEB | sow | |
| MAR | sow | |
| APR | transplant | |
| MAY | harden-off/plant | |
| JUN | grow on | |
| JULY | flowering | |
| AUG | flowering | |
| SEPT | flowering | |
| OCT | flowering | |
| NOV | / | |
| DEC | / | |

RECOMMENDED VARIETIES

*Coreopsis tinctoria:*
'Mahogany Midget'
'T&M Dwarf Mixed'
'T&M Originals Mixed'

*Coreopsis grandiflora:*
'Early Sunrise'
'Gold Star'
'Mayfield Giant'
'Sunburst'

# COSMOS
*Cosmos*

*'SENSATION MIXED' is a tall-growing (90cm/3ft) cosmos with single flowers of red, pink, white and shades in between.*

*DURING THE SUMMER varieties of* Cosmos bipinnatus *grown in borders form masses of feathery leaves topped by flowers.*

## FEATURES

Cosmos, with their finely cut, feathery foliage and large daisy-type flowers grow up to 1.5m (5ft) tall, but shorter varieties are available and can be used in containers. Varieties of *Cosmos bipinnatus* have red, pink, purple or white flowers, while yellow, orange and scarlet are available in varieties of *Cosmos sulphureus*. Cosmos is grown as either a hardy or a half-hardy annual, and is an excellent choice for a cottage garden style border. 'Seashells' has tubular 'fluted' petals, and the taller varieties such as 'Sensation Mixed' are good for cutting.

### COSMOS AT A GLANCE

A hardy or half-hardy annual grown for its large daisy-like flowers. For borders, pots and cutting. Frost hardy to 0°C (32°F).

| | | RECOMMENDED VARIETIES |
|---|---|---|
| JAN | / | *Cosmos bipinnatus:* |
| FEB | / | 'Daydream' |
| MAR | sow 🐾 | 'Gazebo' |
| APR | sow/transplant 🐾 | 'Picotee' |
| MAY | sow/plant 🐾 | 'Seashells/Sea Shells' |
| JUN | flowering 🌸 | 'Sensation Mixed' |
| JULY | flowering 🌸 | 'Sonata Mixed' |
| AUG | flowering 🌸 | *Cosmos sulphureus:* |
| SEPT | flowering 🌸 | 'Ladybird Mixed' |
| OCT | / | 'Ladybird Scarlet' |
| NOV | / | 'Sunny Red' |
| DEC | / | |

## CONDITIONS

**Aspect** Needs full sun to flourish.
**Site** Well-drained soil is essential for success, and good results are guaranteed on light and slightly hungry soils. Pea sticks or twiggy shoots may be needed for support in exposed spots. Any multipurpose compost will give good results in patio pots and containers.

## GROWING METHOD

**Sowing** Raise plants by sowing in March at 16°C (61°F). Sow the long thin seeds in 9cm (3½in) pots of multipurpose compost, then transplant to cell trays and grow on. Harden off at the end of May before planting after frosts, or sow in April/May directly into the ground where plants are to grow. Final spacing between plants should be 15–45cm (6–18in) depending on the variety grown.
**Feeding** Generally not necessary.
**Problems** Slugs will eat young seedlings outdoors so protect with slug pellets.

## FLOWERING

**Season** Flowers appear from early summer onwards.
**Cutting** The taller varieties are ideal as cut flowers. Ensure regular removal of faded flowers.

## AFTER FLOWERING

**General** Pull up plants when frosted, but leaving a few to die off will ensure some self-sown seedlings.

# DAHLIA
*Bedding dahlia*

*BEDDING DAHLIAS usually come in mixed colours. By planting time you can usually separate plants by flower colour.*

*'DOUBLE DELIGHT MIXED' is a popular bedding variety ideally suited for growing in patio containers, reaching 45cm (18in) tall.*

## FEATURES

Seed-raised bedding dahlias are close cousins of the 'border' dahlia grown from tubers. A wide range is available, the dwarfer types growing only 30cm (12in) tall. Flower colour is varied and some like 'Redskin' also have bronze leaves. Grow as half-hardy annuals, and use for bedding displays, patio containers and even windowboxes. Choose from single, double or decorative 'collarette' type flowers. Widely available as young plants.

## CONDITIONS

**Aspect**    Bedding dahlias need full sun all day.
**Site**    Dig in large amounts of decayed manure or compost at least two or three weeks before planting. Soil must be well-drained but moisture-retentive. For containers use multipurpose compost with added slow-release fertiliser granules to keep growth strong through the summer months.

### DAHLIA AT A GLANCE

A half-hardy annual grown for its pretty flowers and an ideal summer bedding or container plant. Frost hardy to ºecC (32ºF).

| | | |
|---|---|---|
| Jan | / | |
| Feb | sow | |
| Mar | sow | |
| Apr | transplant/grow | |
| May | harden off/plant | |
| Jun | flowering | |
| July | flowering | |
| Aug | flowering | |
| Sept | flowering | |
| Oct | flowering | |
| Nov | / | |
| Dec | / | |

RECOMMENDED VARIETIES

**Dahlia hybrids:**
**Taller varieties**
  'Collarette Dandy'
  'Coltness Hybrids Mixed'
  'Pompon Mixed'
**Shorter varieties**
  'Diablo Mixed'
  'Dwarf Double Delight'
  'Dwarf Amore'
  'Figaro Mixed'
  'Redskin'

## GROWING METHOD

**Sowing**    Sow seed February/March in 9cm (3½in) pots and just cover. Water and keep at 16ºC (61ºF) in a light spot. Transplant seedlings when big enough to handle into individual 9cm (3½in) pots and grow on. Harden off at the end of May and plant in early June when all frosts are over, spacing plants 15–30cm (6–12in) apart.

**Feeding**    Water and liquid feed once a week, depending on the soil and weather conditions. Continue watering regularly throughout the season.

**Problems**    Dahlia leaves are eaten by slugs so protect with slug pellets. Flowers may be chewed by earwigs – to catch them fill upturned pots with straw and support these on canes amongst the flowers. Powdery mildew can affect leaves in late summer but is not serious.

## FLOWERING

**Season**    The main show is from midsummer onwards lasting well into autumn until the first frosts.
**Cutting**    Taller varieties of bedding dahlias make useful and long-lived cut flowers.

## AFTER FLOWERING

**General**    Remove plants when the leaves turn black and collapse. Fleshy tubers of favourite plants can be stored dry and frost-free over the winter.

# DELPHINIUM
## Annual delphinium

*'PACIFIC GIANTS MIXED' is a popular variety of delphinium and comes in a range of colours as well as the blue seen here.*

*ANNUAL DELPHINIUMS can be used as 'gap fillers' in mixed borders, and can be left to grow as a permanent feature if required.*

## FEATURES

Certain varieties of delphinium can be grown from seed and treated as half-hardy annuals, even though they are by nature perennials. The flower spikes of up to 1.5m (5ft) are perfect for giving height to summer bedding schemes and are attractive for cutting. Favourite plants can be moved to a permanent position in autumn. Seeds and plants are poisonous.

## CONDITIONS

**Aspect**    Best in full sun.

### DELPHINIUM AT A GLANCE

A perennial treated as a half-hardy annual and grown for its tall spikes of flowers in summer. Frost hardy to −15°C (5°F).

| | | |
|---|---|---|
| JAN | / | |
| FEB | / | |
| MAR | sow | |
| APR | transplant | |
| MAY | grow/plant | |
| JUN | flowering | |
| JULY | flowering | |
| AUG | flowering | |
| SEPT | flowering | |
| OCT | / | |
| NOV | / | |
| DEC | / | |

RECOMMENDED VARIETIES

**Delphinium hybrids:**
  'Connecticut Yankees'
  'Dreaming Spires'
  'Dwarf Pacific Mixed'
  'Dwarf Magic Fountains Mixed'
  'Pacific Giants Mixed'

*Delphinium grandiflorum:*
  'Blue Butterfly'
  'Sky Blue'

**Site**    Delphiniums need shelter from strong winds, and well-drained, moist soil enriched with rotted organic matter before planting. Plants may need support with twiggy sticks or short canes when growing strongly.

## GROWING METHOD

**Sowing**    Sow in pots of multipurpose compost in March at 15°C (60°F), just covering the seeds. Move seedlings into cell trays and grow on in a cold frame or sheltered spot outdoors before planting in May where you want flowers, which appear from midsummer onwards.

**Feeding**    Keep well-watered after planting and liquid feed every 2–3 weeks using a hand-held feeder.

**Problems**    Slugs can decimate young plants in spring so scatter slug pellets or protect with a 5cm (2in) wide band of sharp grit.

## FLOWERING

**Season**    Flowers appear from midsummer onwards.

**Cutting**    For best results cut when the lowest flowers on the spike are fully open and the top buds are starting to show colour.

## AFTER FLOWERING

**General**    If you want to keep certain plants, cut off the foliage as it browns, label them clearly, and then lift and replant when they are fully dormant in late autumn or very early the following spring.

# DIANTHUS BARBATUS
## *Sweet William*

*THE IMPACT OF SWEET WILLIAMS comes from their massed heads of small flowers which often have attractive 'picotee' edges.*

*STRONG SCENT is a characteristic of* Dianthus barbatus *varieties and makes this an ideal plant for cutting in bunches in early summer.*

## FEATURES

Sweet Williams are varieties of *Dianthus barbatus* and have flowers in pink, white, red, burgundy and bicolours, on large rounded heads. Individual flowers often have darker central 'eyes'. Plants have clumping growth up to 45cm (18in), while dwarf forms grow to just 15cm (6in). The flowers appear from spring into early summer and are scented and ideal for cutting. Easily grown from seed as a hardy biennial, and useful for bedding schemes and as blocks of spring colour in mixed borders. Some less common varieties like 'Sooty' have dark, almost black flowers.

### DIANTHUS AT A GLANCE

A summer-sown biennial grown for its large heads of scented flowers in spring and early summer. Frost hardy to −15°C (5°F).

| | | |
|---|---|---|
| JAN | / | |
| FEB | / | |
| MAR | / | |
| APR | flowering 🌿 | |
| MAY | flowers/sow 🌿🌿 | |
| JUN | flowers/sow 🌿🌿 | |
| JULY | flowering 🌿 | |
| AUG | grow on 🌿 | |
| SEPT | grow on 🌿 | |
| OCT | plant 🌿 | |
| NOV | / | |
| DEC | / | |

RECOMMENDED VARIETIES

*Dianthus barbatus:*
**Tall varieties**
  'Auricula-Eyed Mixed'
  'Forerunner Mixed'
  'Gemstones'
  'Harlequin'
  'Monarch Mixed'
**Dwarf varieties**
  'Dwarf Mixed'
  'Indian Carpet Mixed'

## CONDITIONS

**Aspect**  Grow sweet Williams in full sun.
**Site**  Needs well-drained soil that has been limed before planting, and has had plenty of rotted compost mixed in several weeks before.

## GROWING METHOD

**Sowing**  Sow the fine seed in rows outdoors, 1cm (½in) deep and just cover, in May/June. Transplant the seedlings so they are in rows 15cm (6in) apart and pinch out the growing tips to make them bushy. Water regularly throughout the summer months, and then lift and plant in their flowering positions in October, keeping the roots intact. For cut flowers only, the plants can be left growing in rows.
**Feeding**  Liquid feed monthly during the summer.
**Problems**  Poor drainage during winter can kill plants. If leaves are attacked by rust disease try a spray containing the fungicide penconazole.

## FLOWERING

**Season**  Flowers appear from late spring to early summer and it is possible to get a second 'flush' if all the stalks are cut hard back after the first flowers have faded.
**Cutting**  An excellent cut flower, and ideal for making into a rounded 'posy'.

## AFTER FLOWERING

**General**  Pull plants up when they are past their best, or leave some to develop into bigger clumps.

# DIANTHUS CHINENSIS

## Chinese pink

*AS CONTAINER PLANTS Chinese pinks are perfect as neat edging plants, all growing to the same height. They are also valuable as colourful fillers and effectively bridge the gap between taller plants in the centre of large tubs and trailing plants falling over the edges.*

## FEATURES

Growing 20–30cm (8–12in) high, varieties of *Dianthus chinensis* are suitable for massed planting, edging garden beds, or for use in troughs or pots. Chinese pink is grown as a half-hardy annual although it is fully hardy outdoors. Flower are red, pink or white with only slight scent. Available as young plants.

## CONDITIONS

**Aspect**     Needs full sun to flower at its best.

### DIANTHUS AT A GLANCE

A hardy annual grown for its small brightly coloured 'pink' type flowers, used in bedding/pots. Frost hardy to –15°C (5°F).

| | | RECOMMENDED VARIETIES |
|---|---|---|
| JAN | / | *Dianthus chinensis:* |
| FEB | / | 'Baby Doll Mixed' |
| MAR | sow | 'Black & White |
| APR | transplant | Minstrels' |
| MAY | harden off/plant | 'Double Gaiety Mixed' |
| JUN | flowering | 'Princess Mixed' |
| JULY | flowering | 'Raspberry Parfait' |
| AUG | flowering | 'Snowfire' |
| SEPT | flowering | 'Strawberry Parfait' |
| OCT | / | 'T&M Frosty Mixed' |
| NOV | / | |
| DEC | / | |

**Site**     Needs well-drained soil, but dig in plenty of well-rotted manure or compost when preparing beds. Lime can be added to the soil before planting and raked in. Containers must have very good drainage.

## GROWING METHOD

**Sowing**     Sow seeds in 9cm (3½in) pots of multipurpose compost in March, just cover, and keep at 15°C (60°F) in a light place. When seedlings are 2.5cm (1in) tall, transplant to cell trays and grow on with some protection (a cold-frame is suitable). Harden off at the end of May and plant out in beds or containers.

**Feeding**     Do not overwater – a good weekly watering should be sufficient, and feed with liquid feed every 2–3 weeks. Plants in containers need no extra feeding if slow-release fertiliser is added.

**Problems**     Overwatering will cause yellowing of the leaves and rotting off at soil/compost level.

## FLOWERING

**Season**     Plants come into flower from early summer onwards and will continue until autumn if dead flowerheads are removed regularly.

**Cutting**     Taller varieties can be used as cut flowers, but choose a variety known for its scent such as 'Double Gaiety Mixed'.

## AFTER FLOWERING

**General**     Remove plants when finished and compost.

# DIGITALIS
*Foxglove*

*FOXGLOVES are perfect for cottage-style borders and make good companions for the red poppies and white lavatera.*

*WHITE FOXGLOVES are useful for a specific colour scheme – this is a white-flowered plant of the 'Excelsior Hybrids'.*

## FEATURES

Varieties of *Digitalis purpurea* grow up to 2m (6ft) tall with spikes of tubular pink, white, magenta, cream or purple flowers, each with a spotted lip. Plant in groups in borders or in a partly-shaded spot under trees. All parts of the plant are poisonous, including the seeds. Grow as a hardy biennial, although the variety 'Foxy' can be treated as an annual and sown in spring.

## CONDITIONS

**Aspect**     Succeeds in part or dappled shade, or in sun.

### DIGITALIS AT A GLANCE

A hardy biennial grown for tall spikes of flowers appearing in early summer. Useful for shade. Frost hardy to −15°C (5°F).

| | | |
|---|---|---|
| JAN | / | |
| FEB | / | |
| MAR | / | |
| APR | sow | |
| MAY | sow/transplant | |
| JUN | sow/flowers | |
| JULY | flowering | |
| AUG | grow | |
| SEPT | grow | |
| OCT | plant | |
| NOV | / | |
| DEC | / | |

RECOMMENDED VARIETIES

*Digitalis purpurea:*
 'Alba'
 'Excelsior Hybrids'
 'Foxy Mixed'
 'Giant Spotted Mixed'
 'Glittering Prizes Mixed'
 'Selected Mixed'
 'Suttons Apricot'

**Site**     Soil needs to be free-draining and enriched with organic matter well ahead of planting – use rotted compost or manure in generous amounts. Staking is necessary when plants are grown in a position exposed to winds.

## GROWING METHOD

**Sowing**     Sow the very small seed in a 9cm (3½in) pot and barely cover, from April–June. Keep outside in a coldframe or sheltered spot, and transplant seedlings individually to 9cm (3½in) pots. Grow on through the summer, potting on into 12.5cm (5in) pots when roots fill the smaller pots. Plant out in October where you want the plants to flower. The variety 'Foxy' can be sown in February in warmth and planted in May for flowers the same summer. Treat as a half-hardy annual.

**Feeding**     Feed fortnightly with liquid feed while plants are in pots and do not allow to dry out. Water in spring during dry spells as growth begins.

**Problems**     No special problems affect foxgloves.

## FLOWERING

**Season**     Flowers appear in early summer.

**Cutting**     Not particularly good as a cut flower.

## AFTER FLOWERING

**General**     Once stems have flowered, cut them off just above the leaves and plants may then produce several shorter flowering stems. Leave a few spikes to set seed pods which will self-seed.

# DOROTHEANTHUS

*Mesembryanthemum or Livingstone daisy*

*LIVINGSTONE DAISIES set beds alight with colour on bright sunny days when the flowers open fully. Planted 15cm (6in) apart each way they soon knit together to create a tapestry of colour, and look especially at home when creeping amongst pieces of stone on a sunny rock garden.*

## FEATURES

Mesembryanthemum, also known as Livingstone daisy, is ideal for planting on dry, sunny banks, on rockeries, and in pots of free-draining compost. It has a spreading habit, but is only 15cm (6in) tall at most. The fleshy leaves have a crystalline texture with bright, daisy-like flowers in many shades. Grow as a half-hardy annual. All varieties of *Dorotheanthus bellidiformis* have the habit of closing their flowers in dull and wet spells of weather, opening again in bright sunshine.

### DOROTHEANTHUS AT A GLANCE

A half-hardy, spreading annual grown for its daisy-like flowers which open fully in sunshine. Frost hardy to 0°C (32°F).

| | | |
|---|---|---|
| JAN | / | |
| FEB | / | |
| MAR | sow | |
| APR | sow/transplant | |
| MAY | plant/harden off | |
| JUN | flowering | |
| JULY | flowering | |
| AUG | flowering | |
| SEPT | flowering | |
| OCT | / | |
| NOV | / | |
| DEC | / | |

RECOMMENDED VARIETIES

*Dorotheanthus bellidiformis:*
 'Gelato Pink'
 'Harlequin Mixed'
 'Lunette' ('Yellow Ice')
 'Magic Carpet Mixed'
 'Sparkles'

## CONDITIONS

**Aspect** Needs full direct sun all day and will perform even better on a south-facing sloping bank.

**Site** Needs very well drained soil, with no special soil preparation necessary as plants grow better on light, sandy and hungry soils. If grown in containers used soil-based compost and mix with fifty per cent grit for good drainage.

## GROWING METHOD

**Sowing** Sow seed in a 9cm (3½in) pot of soil-based seed compost in March and barely cover. Keep at 18°C (64°F) in a light spot. When seedlings are large enough transplant to cell trays of soil-based potting compost and grow on. Harden off at the end of May for two weeks and plant after the last frosts 15cm (6in) apart.

**Feeding** Extra feeding is unnecessary and produces leaves at the expense of flowers. Take care not to overwater in beds or pots or plants will rot.

**Problems** Slugs will attack the fleshy young leaves so scatter slug pellets after planting out.

## FLOWERING

**Season** Flowers appear from midsummer onwards. Remove faded flowers to encourage more.

**Cutting** Not suitable for cutting.

## AFTER FLOWERING

**General** Pull up and compost when finished.

# ESCHSCHOLZIA
## *California poppy*

*AUTUMN SOWING of eschscholzia will produce early spring flowers around the same time as this bright green* Euphorbia polychroma.

*DRY, HOT, SUN-BAKED banks are perfect for California poppies, where conditions are very like those of their native America.*

## FEATURES

The bright flowers and finely divided blue-green foliage of the California poppy are best in large drifts, although it grows well even in cracks in paving and in gravel, and thrives on dry soils in full sun. Varieties of *Eschscholzia californica* have flowers in yellow, cream, pink/beige, apricot and scarlet. They grow 30cm (12in) tall and wide. Grow as a hardy annual, sowing where plants are to flower. Very easy to grow and quickly self-seeds.

## CONDITIONS

**Aspect**      Eschscholzia thrives in hot, sun-baked spots

**Site**      where other annuals struggle to grow. Must have full sun and likes it hot. Poor light soil often gives the best results, as long as drainage is good. No special soil preparation is necessary, and avoid adding compost or manure which encourages leafy growth at the expense of flowers.

## GROWING METHOD

**Sowing**      Sow in March or September outdoors where plants are to flower as it dislikes being transplanted. Spread seed thinly in short drills 1cm (½in) deep and cover. Thin seedlings as they grow to allow 7.5–15cm (3–6in) between plants. Water thoroughly after thinning to settle plants back in.

**Feeding**      Except in spells of drought, watering is not necessary, and extra feed is not required.

**Problems**      No particular problems.

## FLOWERING

**Season**      Long flowering period through the spring and summer months if faded flowers are removed.

**Cutting**      Use as a cut flower, although flowers close at night. Cut long stems and place in water immediately to just below the flower buds.

## AFTER FLOWERING

**General**      Often self-seeds, so seedlings can be expected the following season. These will appear in cracks in paving, along paths and drives and in gravel, where they are perfectly at home in dry, poor soil conditions.

### ESCHSCHOLZIA AT A GLANCE

A hardy annual grown for its bright poppy-like flowers and ideal for light, dry soils and along paths. Frost hardy to −15°C (5°F).

| | | RECOMMENDED VARIETIES |
|---|---|---|
| JAN | / | *Eschscholzia californica:* |
| FEB | / | 'Apricot Bush' |
| MAR | sow | 'Apricot Chiffon' |
| APR | thin out | 'Apricot Flambeau' |
| MAY | thin out | 'Dalli' |
| JUN | flowering | 'Mission Bells Mixed' |
| JULY | flowering | 'Prima Ballerina' |
| AUG | flowering | 'Rose Bush' |
| SEPT | flowers/sow | 'Thai Silk Mixed' |
| OCT | / | *Eschscholzia lobbii:* |
| NOV | / | 'Moonlight' |
| DEC | / | |

# EUPHORBIA

*Snow-on-the-mountain*

*THE COLOUR of snow-on-the-mountain comes from the white-edged leaves and this becomes more intense near the tops of the plants.*

*WHEN GROWN IN POTS Euphorbia marginata can be planted in mixed borders in groups of 3–5 plants for cool splashes of colour.*

## FEATURES

Commonly known as snow-on-the-mountain, *Euphorbia marginata* is grown for its attractive leaves. The flowers are insignificant, but the leaves have an edging of white. Plants grow 60–90cm (2–3ft) tall and are used in annual or mixed borders. Grow as a hardy annual. The milky sap is poisonous.

## CONDITIONS

**Aspect**     Needs to be grown in the open in full sun.

### EUPHORBIA AT A GLANCE

A hardy annual grown for its attractive leaves which are streaked and edged with white. Frost hardy to –5°C (23°F).

| | | RECOMMENDED VARIETIES |
|---|---|---|
| JAN | / | |
| FEB | / | *Euphorbia marginata:* |
| MAR | sow | 'Summer Icicle' |
| APR | thin out | |
| MAY | thin out | |
| JUN | flowering | |
| JULY | flowering | |
| AUG | flowering | |
| SEPT | flowering | |
| OCT | / | |
| NOV | / | |
| DEC | / | |

**Site**     Does not tolerate poor drainage and succeeds best on light and slightly hungry soils – sandy soils give good results. Add very well-rotted organic matter before planting to help retain soil moisture.

## GROWING METHOD

**Sowing**     Sow seed during March direct into the ground where plants are to grow, which avoids root disturbance as they develop. Make short drills 1cm (½in) deep and scatter seed thinly, then cover. Plants are gradually thinned out so that final spacing is 15–30cm (6–12in) by early summer. In exposed gardens short twigs can be used as supports. Alternatively, sow in pots in a coldframe and transplant to cell trays, planting out in May.

**Feeding**     Grows well without extra feeding.
**Problems**     Trouble-free.

## FLOWERING

**Season**     From early summer onwards.
**Cutting**     Foliage may be used in arrangements but stems must be burnt or scalded to stop the milky sap bleeding. Wear gloves to avoid getting the irritant sap on skin.

## AFTER FLOWERING

**General**     Remove plants in late summer and autumn when they are past their best, but leave a few to die down and self-seed into the soil.

# GAZANIA
## *Gazania*

GAZANIA *flowers often have striking darker markings toward their centres.*

IN MILD SEASIDE GARDENS *it is worth leaving gazanias out during the winter months as they often survive unharmed and will give an early show of flowers the following spring.*

## FEATURES

Gazanias come in an amazing range of brilliant colours from pastel pinks to cream, strong reds and mahogany. Modern varieties with striped petals are very eye-catching. All have contrasting 'eyes' to the flowers. Gazanias are grown as half-hardy annuals from spring-sown seeds and used in beds and patio pots. Flowers tend to close up in dull weather, but newer varieties like 'Daybreak Bright Orange' stay open longer. They grow up to 30cm (12in) tall and wide and thrive in seaside gardens.

## CONDITIONS

**Aspect**     For the flowers to open reliably gazanias must be grown where they get baking sun all day.

### GAZANIA AT A GLANCE

A half-hardy annual grown for its bright flowers that open fully in sun. Use in beds and containers. Frost hardy to –5°C (23°F).

| | | RECOMMENDED VARIETIES |
|---|---|---|
| JAN | / | *Gazania rigens:* |
| FEB | / | 'Chansonette' |
| MAR | sow | 'Chansonette Pink Shades' |
| APR | transplant | 'Daybreak Bright Orange' |
| MAY | harden off/plant | 'Daybreak Red Stripe' |
| JUN | flowering | 'Harlequin Hybrids' |
| JULY | flowering | 'Mini Star Mixed' |
| AUG | flowering | 'Sundance Mixed' |
| SEPT | flowering | 'Talent' |
| OCT | / | |
| NOV | / | |
| DEC | / | |

**Site**     Needs well-drained soil that is not too rich or leafy growth is the result. Light sandy soils give the best results. If growing in patio containers, choose clay pots or troughs and use a soil-based compost with extra sharp grit mixed in to ensure good drainage at all times.

## GROWING METHOD

**Sowing**     Seed is sown in March at 20°C (68°F) in a heated propagator, in 9cm (3½in) pots. Just cover the seeds and keep in a light spot. Seedlings appear in 1–2 weeks and can be transplanted when large enough into cell trays. Grow on in a greenhouse or conservatory, then harden off and plant in late May, spacing plants 30cm (12in) apart. In mixed containers make sure they are not shaded out by other plants growing nearby.

**Feeding**     Only water when the soil or compost becomes dry, and stand patio pots under cover during prolonged spells of summer rain.

**Problems**     No real problems, but slugs may attack leaves in wet weather, so protect with slug pellets.

## FLOWERING

**Season**     The flowering period lasts throughout summer if dead flowers and their stalks are removed.

**Cutting**     Flowers are not suitable for cutting.

## AFTER FLOWERING

**General**     Favourite plants can be lifted, potted up and kept dry in a frost-free greenhouse over winter. Cuttings can be taken in spring and new plants grown on for planting out.

# GODETIA
*Godetia*

*FOR A RAINBOW of summer colour sow a mixed variety of godetia that includes shades of rose, pink and white flowers.*

*AT ITS PEAK godetia is smothered in masses of bright flowers with large petals that have a texture similar to crepe paper.*

## FEATURES

Godetia is available in a wide range of varieties and many colours. This hardy annual can be spring- or autumn-sown, the latter giving earlier flowers on bigger plants. Size ranges from 20–90cm (8–36in), with the taller varieties being ideal for cutting. Don't fuss over godetia – the best flowers are produced on slightly hungry, dry soils.

### GODETIA AT A GLANCE

Grown for its bright single or double flowers, this hardy annual can be spring- or autumn-sown. Frost hardy to −15°C (5°F).

| | | RECOMMENDED VARIETIES |
|---|---|---|
| JAN | / | |
| FEB | / | **Godetia hybrids:** |
| MAR | sow | **Tall varieties** |
| APR | sow | 'Duke of York' |
| MAY | thin out | 'Grace Mixed' |
| JUN | flowering | 'Schamini Carmine' |
| JULY | flowering | 'Sybil Sherwood' |
| AUG | flowering | **Dwarf varieties** |
| SEPT | flowers/sow | 'Charivari' |
| OCT | / | 'Lilac Pixie' |
| NOV | / | 'Precious Gems' |
| DEC | / | 'Salmon Princess' |

## CONDITIONS

**Aspect**   Needs an open position in full sun.
**Site**   Needs perfect drainage, but not rich soil.

## GROWING METHOD

**Sowing**   Sow where plants are to grow, just covering the seeds in shallow drills 15cm (6in) apart during March/April, or during September. Thin seedlings until they are 15–30cm (6–12in) apart depending on variety. Do not thin autumn-sown plants until the following spring to allow for winter losses.
**Feeding**   Not needed, or excessive leafy growth results.
**Problems**   Overwatering quickly causes root rot then collapse and death of plants.

## FLOWERING

**Season**   Flowers appear from May onwards on plants sown the previous autumn. Spring-sown plants start flowering from June.
**Cutting**   Excellent cut flower, especially if the taller varieties such as 'Schamini Carmine' and 'Grace Mixed' are grown in rows.

## AFTER FLOWERING

**General**   Remove plants when flowering is over. A few can be left to self-seed onto the soil.

# GOMPHRENA
## *Globe amaranth*

'STRAWBERRY FIELDS' is a large-growing variety of gomphrena with red flowers 5cm (2in) across, on stems 75cm (30in) tall.

GLOBE AMARANTH makes a good edging for paths – choose one of the lower-growing varieties such as 'Gemini Mixed' at 60cm (2ft).

## FEATURES

Also commonly known as bachelor's buttons, gomphrena is a half-hardy annual growing 30–75cm (12–30in) tall depending on the variety. Its rounded heads of purple, pink, white, red and mauve flowers are used in bedding displays and for cutting and drying. 'Strawberry Fields' has bright red flowers.

### GOMPHRENA AT A GLANCE

A half-hardy annual grown for its clover-like flowerheads, used in bedding and for cutting. Frost hardy to 0°C (32°F).

| | | |
|---|---|---|
| JAN | / | |
| FEB | / | |
| MAR | sow | |
| APR | transplant | |
| MAY | harden off/plant | |
| JUN | flowering | |
| JULY | flowering | |
| AUG | flowering | |
| SEPT | flowering | |
| OCT | / | |
| NOV | / | |
| DEC | / | |

RECOMMENDED VARIETIES

*Gomphrena globosa:*
 'Buddy'
 'Full Series'
 'Gemini Mixed'
 'Globe Amaranth'
 'Qis Mixed'

*Gomphrena hybrid:*
 'Strawberry Fields'

## CONDITIONS

**Aspect**  Must have a sunny spot.
**Site**  Needs well-drained soil enriched with rotted manure or compost.

## GROWING METHOD

**Sowing**  Sow in March in 9cm (3½in) pots of multipurpose compost, just covering the seeds (soaking for a few days before helps germination). Keep at 18°C (64°F) in a warm, dark place such as an airing cupboard and check regularly – seedlings appear in about two weeks. Transplant into cell trays, grow on under cover, harden off in late May, and plant out after frosts, 25–30cm (10–12in) apart.
**Feeding**  Give an all-purpose liquid feed monthly.
**Problems**  No special problems affect gomphrena.

## FLOWERING

**Season**  Flowers appear from midsummer to autumn.
**Cutting**  Used fresh as a cut flower, but can also be dried in late summer by hanging upside down in a warm, dry, airy place.

## AFTER FLOWERING

**General**  Pull up in autumn and use for composting.

# GYPSOPHILA

*Baby's breath*

*CLOUDS OF SMALL FLOWERS are produced on annual gypsophila all summer if a few seeds are sown at two-week intervals from April until early June. For cut flowers grow plants in a spare corner because they look bare once you begin to regularly remove stems.*

## FEATURES

Hardy annual varieties of *Gypsophila elegans* grow up to 60cm (2ft) tall and wide with many-divided stems bearing small, dainty pink, white or rose flowers. It is widely used in flower arranging and as a 'foil' for other plants in summer bedding schemes. The dwarf-growing *Gypsophila muralis* 'Garden Bride', at 15cm (6in), is ideal for baskets and containers.

## CONDITIONS

**Aspect**    Grow gypsophila in full sun.

### GYPSOPHILA AT A GLANCE

Gypsophila is a hardy annual grown for tall, much branching stems of flowers, for beds/cutting. Frost hardy to −15°C (5°F).

| | | RECOMMENDED VARIETIES |
|---|---|---|
| JAN | / | *Gypsophila elegans:* |
| FEB | / | 'Bright Rose' |
| MAR | / | 'Colour Blend' |
| APR | sow | 'Covent Garden' |
| MAY | thin out | 'Kermesina' |
| JUN | flowering | 'Monarch White' |
| JULY | flowering | 'Rosea' |
| AUG | flowering | 'Snow Fountain' |
| SEPT | flowers/sow | 'White Elephant' |
| OCT | / | *Gypsophila muralis:* |
| NOV | / | 'Garden Bride' |
| DEC | / | |

**Site**    Rotted compost or manure should be dug in before planting, for strong plants and better flowers, but the soil must also be well-drained. Varieties grown in baskets and containers will succeed in any multipurpose compost.

## GROWING METHOD

**Sowing**    Seeds can go straight into the ground where plants will grow and flower. Sow in short drills 1cm (½in) deep in April, then thin to finally leave plants 10–15cm (4–6in) apart to give each other support and allow room to grow. September sowing produces stronger plants with earlier flowers the following spring – do not thin out until after winter.

**Feeding**    Feeding is not generally necessary if the soil has been well prepared beforehand. In dry spells give the soil a thorough soaking, and do not let containers dry out.

**Problems**    Gypsophila is trouble-free, but young plants are prone to rotting off on heavy soils.

## FLOWERING

**Season**    Flowers appear from June onwards on spring-sown plants, several weeks earlier on those sown the previous autumn.

**Cutting**    Excellent when cut and an ideal 'filler' to marry together other flowers in a wide range of floral arrangements.

## AFTER FLOWERING

**General**    Pull up plants and use for composting.

# HELIANTHUS
## *Sunflower*

*SUNFLOWERS have a central 'disc' which eventually becomes the fat seedhead in autumn and makes useful food for the birds.*

*'PACINO' is a modern variety of* Helianthus annuus, *small enough to be used in patio pots, growing to only 45cm (18in) tall.*

## FEATURES

Sunflowers range in height from 45cm (18in) up to 5m (15ft) depending on the variety grown. They can be used in bedding, in patio containers, as cut flowers, or can be grown as traditional 'giants' to several metres (feet) tall. Plants produce single or multi-flowered heads and the colour range is enormous. 'Teddy Bear' has furry, double flowers. Annual sunflowers are fully hardy and flower from mid-summer onwards. Certain varieties such as 'Prado Sun & Fire' have been bred to be pollen-free and these are ideal for use as indoor cut flowers. Seedheads left in the garden in autumn provide food for birds.

## CONDITIONS

**Aspect**    Must have an open position in full sun.

### HELIANTHUS AT A GLANCE

A hardy annual grown for its large flowers on both dwarf and tall plants; some are ideal for cutting. Frost hardy to −15°C (5°F).

| | | RECOMMENDED VARIETIES |
|---|---|---|
| JAN | / | *Helianthus annuus:* |
| FEB | / | **Tall varieties** |
| MAR | sow |   'Italian White' |
| APR | thin out |   'Pastiche' |
| MAY | support |   'Velvet Queen' |
| JUN | flowering | **For containers** |
| JULY | flowering |   'Big Smile' |
| AUG | flowering |   'Pacino' |
| SEPT | flowering | **Double flowers** |
| OCT | / |   'Orange Sun' |
| NOV | / |   'Sungold Double' |
| DEC | / |   'Teddy Bear' |

**Site**    Tolerates most soil conditions but soil enriched with plenty of manure or compost makes growth both rapid and vigorous, producing the largest flowerheads. Plants grown in groups in borders tend to support each other, but in exposed spots tie tall varieties to a cane. Use multipurpose compost mixed with slow-release fertiliser for planting up patio containers and windowboxes.

## GROWING METHOD

**Sowing**    Seeds are large and easy to handle – sow three seeds outdoors where plants are to grow in March, removing all but the strongest when 15cm (6in) tall. Can also be sown three seeds to a 9cm (3½in) pot of compost and treated in the same way. Pot-grown plants can be kept outdoors and planted when the roots fill the pot. Spacing depends on the variety grown.

**Feeding**    Extra feeding is not usually needed but keep plants well watered in long dry spells.

**Problems**    Slugs and snails can attack young plants cutting them off at ground level, so protect with slug pellets or a barrier of sharp grit.

## FLOWERING

**Season**    Throughout summer and early autumn.

**Cutting**    A very good cut flower but use a heavy vase or add some weight to the bottom of it to prevent it toppling over. Pollen-free varieties should be grown if allergies are a known problem.

## AFTER FLOWERING

**General**    Leave the seedheads as bird food during autumn and winter, and then dig out the extensive roots. Sunflower roots can help break-up and loosen heavy, compacted soils.

# HELICHRYSUM
*Strawflower*

*FOR DRYING cut helichrysum before the flowers reach this stage, while the petals are still curved inwards (bottom right).*

*PAPER DAISIES ARE APT to be rather leggy, but the range of flower colours can be stunning, as shown here.*

## FEATURES

Varieties of strawflower come from *Helichrysum bracteatum*, with plants growing 15–60cm (6–24in) tall. They are among the easiest annuals to grow for dried flowers, with double blooms in many colours, and petals that feel straw-like. Dwarf varieties make long-lasting container plants. A half-hardy annual.

## CONDITIONS

**Aspect**     Must have a warm spot in full sun.

### HELICHRYSUM AT A GLANCE

A half-hardy annual grown for its long-lasting dried flowers, and also used in bedding and containers. Frost hardy to 0°C (32°F).

| | | |
|---|---|---|
| JAN | / | |
| FEB | / | |
| MAR | sow | |
| APR | transplant/grow | |
| MAY | harden off/plant | |
| JUN | flowering | |
| JULY | flowering | |
| AUG | flowering | |
| SEPT | flowers/cutting | |
| OCT | flowers/cutting | |
| NOV | / | |
| DEC | / | |

RECOMMENDED VARIETIES

*Helichrysum bracteatum:*
**Tall varieties**
'Drakkar Pastel Mixed'
'Monstrosum Double Mixed'
'Pastel Mixed'
'Swiss Giants'
**Dwarf varieties**
'Bright Bikini'
'Chico Mixed'
'Hot Bikini'

**Site**     Needs very well-drained soil that has been enriched with rotted compost or manure. If growing in containers use multipurpose compost and add slow-release fertiliser. Tall varieties will need staking as they develop.

## GROWING METHOD

**Sowing**     Sow seeds in March in 9cm (3½in) pots of multipurpose compost and germinate at 18°C (64°F). Transplant seedlings to cell trays when large enough and grow on, then harden off at the end of May and plant 15–60cm (6–24in) apart depending on the variety. Seed can also be sown direct into short drills in the soil during May and the young plants gradually thinned to the planting distances above. In containers pack 2–3 plants together in groups to get a good block of flower colour.

**Feeding**     Helichrysum grows well without extra feeding, but water container-grown plants regularly.

**Problems**     By late summer the leaves are often attacked by mildew, but it is not worth treating.

## FLOWERING

**Season**     Flowers appear from early to midsummer.
**Cutting**     Pick the flowers when the petals are still incurved. Hang the bunches upside down in a dry, airy place to dry out. Long-lasting.

## AFTER FLOWERING

**General**     Cut what you want and then pull up.

# HELIPTERUM
## *Everlasting daisy*

*WHEN PLANTS REACH this stage of growth the entire plant can be harvested and hung up to dry. Individual stems are then cut off.*

*THINNING PLANTS to 15–30cm (6–12in) apart helps them support each other. The flowers have a distinct rustle in a breeze.*

## FEATURES

The papery flowers of everlasting daisies come mainly in pinks and white. They grow 30–45cm (12–18in) tall, and can be used in bedding or cut for dried flower arrangements. In catalogues they are also found listed under acrolinium and rhodanthe. Hardy annual.

## CONDITIONS

**Aspect**  These Australian natives need full sun.
**Site**  Helipterum must have perfectly drained soil

| HELIPTERUM AT A GLANCE | | |
|---|---|---|
| A half–hardy annual grown for its pinkish, 'papery' flowers that are good for cutting and drying. Frost hardy to 0°C (32°F). | | |
| JAN | / | RECOMMENDED VARIETIES |
| FEB | / | Helipterum hybrids: |
| MAR | / | 'Bonny' |
| APR | sow | 'Double Mixed' |
| MAY | sow/thin | 'Goliath' |
| JUN | flowering | 'Pierrot' |
| JULY | flowering | 'Special Mixed' |
| AUG | flowers/cutting | |
| SEPT | flowers/cutting | |
| OCT | / | |
| NOV | / | |
| DEC | / | |

and does not require special preparation – the best results are obtained on thin and hungry soils which mimic the plant's natural growing conditions. Sheltered hot-spots are best.

## GROWING METHOD

**Sowing**  Sow seeds direct into the soil in short drills 1cm (½in) deep and 15cm (6in) apart in April and May. Thin the seedlings as they grow, so plants are eventually 15–30cm (6–12in) apart by early summer. Water only during long dry spells, but this is not necessary once flower buds begin to appear.
**Feeding**  Do not feed.
**Problems**  Plants fail on heavy, wet soils that are slow to warm up in spring, so try growing them in raised beds which have better drainage.

## FLOWERING

**Season**  Although the plants flower for only a brief spell the effect is long-lasting because of their 'everlasting' nature.
**Cutting**  Ideal as cut, dried flower. For the best results cut off whole plants when most of the flowers are still just opening out, and hang upside down in a dry, airy place.

## AFTER FLOWERING

**General**  Plants sometimes self-seed. Any plants not lifted for drying are pulled up in autumn and added to the compost heap.

# IBERIS
## *Candytuft*

*CANDYTUFT is available in a wide range of colourful mixtures. Each 5cm (2in) wide 'flower' is actually a mass of smaller flowers.*

*ALL SORTS OF COLOURS appear in varieties of Iberis umbellata, including white as seen here. The flowers have a sweet fragrance.*

## FEATURES

Very decorative plants that grow no more than 30cm (12in) tall, varieties of *Iberis umbellata*, a hardy annual, have sweet-scented flowers in white, pink, mauve, red and purple. They produce good results even in poor soils and quickly self-seed so you get new plants springing up every year, which are at home growing in-between paving and in gravel drives. The best plants with the most flowers come from sowing in early spring.

## CONDITIONS

**Aspect**
**Site**

Iberis prefers an open spot in full sun. Although it is happy in poor soil, adding rotted manure or compost before planting will help keep moisture in and reduce the need for extra watering during summer.

### IBERIS AT A GLANCE

Iberis is a hardy annual grown for its heads of bright, scented flowers which are used in bedding. Frost hardy to –15°C (5°F).

| | | |
|---|---|---|
| JAN | / | |
| FEB | / | |
| MAR | sow | |
| APR | sow | |
| MAY | thin out | |
| JUN | flowering | |
| JULY | flowering | |
| AUG | flowering | |
| SEPT | sow | |
| OCT | / | |
| NOV | / | |
| DEC | / | |

**RECOMMENDED VARIETIES**

*Iberis umbellata:*
 'Dwarf Fairy Mixed'
 'Fantasia Mixed'
 'Flash Mixed'
 'Spangles'

## GROWING METHOD

**Sowing**

Seed is sown outdoors in March/April where the plants are to flower. Mark out circular patches of ground with sand and make short parallel drills 1cm (½in) deep inside the circle, spaced 15cm (6in) apart. Sow the seeds thinly in these drills and cover with fine, raked soil. Seedlings appear in 2–3 weeks and should be thinned out so they are eventually 7.5–15cm (3–6in) apart by early summer. Can also be sown in September for earlier flowers.

**Feeding**

Extra feeding is not necessary. Watering in early summer will stop plants flowering prematurely before they achieve a good size.

**Problems**

Being relatives of brassicas like cabbage, they can suffer from clubroot disease. Treatment is not worthwhile, but to continue to enjoy candytuft where clubroot is present, sow a pinch of seed in 9cm (3½in) pots of multi-purpose compost in early spring and plant out clumps in early summer. Disease-free roots will support the plants and let them flower.

## FLOWERING

**Season**
**Cutting**

Flowers will appear from early summer.
Good cut flower. Flowers that are well formed but not over-mature should last well if picked early in the day and immediately plunged into water to soak before arranging.

## AFTER FLOWERING

**General**

Plants can be cut down after flowering, given a good soak with liquid feed, and they will usually produce a second 'flush' of flowerheads several weeks later. Candytuft self-seeds very easily so leave a few plants to die away naturally and scatter their seeds. Seed can also be collected for sowing the following spring.

# IMPATIENS

## *Busy lizzie*

VIGOROUS AND LARGE-FLOWERED, 'Accent Mixed' will carpet the ground in borders or fill containers in sun or shade.

NEW GUINEA busy lizzies can be successfully combined with smaller flowered varieties like this delightful 'Mosaic Lilac'.

## FEATURES

Impatiens perform well in sun or shade and a huge range is available. Use in bedding, tubs, windowboxes, hanging baskets and flower bags. As well as busy lizzies, there are also the larger 'New Guinea' types (30cm/12in), and the 'balsams', with bushy growth (25cm/10in). Busy lizzies grow from 15–30cm (6–12in) tall and wide depending on variety. All impatiens are half-hardy annuals, and raising from seed requires some care. Widely available as young plants by mail order, they can also be bought ready-grown in spring. Flowers can be single or double in mixed or various colours.

### IMPATIENS AT A GLANCE

A half-hardy annual grown for its flowers for bedding, containers and hanging planters. Frost hardy to 0°C (32°F).

| | | |
|---|---|---|
| JAN | / | |
| FEB | sow | |
| MAR | sow | |
| APR | grow on | |
| MAY | harden/plant | |
| JUN | flowering | |
| JULY | flowering | |
| AUG | flowering | |
| SEPT | flowering | |
| OCT | flowering | |
| NOV | / | |
| DEC | / | |

RECOMMENDED VARIETIES

**Busy lizzies:**
 'Accent Mixed'
 'Bruno'
 'Mosaic Rose'
 'Super Elfin Mixed'
**New Guinea impatiens:**
 'Firelake Mixed'
 'Spectra'
 'Tango'
*Impatiens balsamifera:*
 'Tom Thumb Mixed'

## CONDITIONS

**Aspect** Will succeed in full sun or moderate shade.
**Site** Soil should have rotted manure or compost mixed in before planting, and should be well-drained. Avoid planting in windy spots. In containers and baskets use multipurpose compost with slow-release fertiliser added.

## GROWING METHOD

**Sowing** In late February/March sow seeds onto a fine layer of vermiculite in 9cm (3½in) pots of seed compost. Tap to settle but do not cover. Seal in a clear plastic bag or put in a heated propagator, in a bright place at 21–24°C (70–75°F). Seedlings appear in 2–3 weeks and are transplanted to cell trays when 2.5cm (1in) tall. Grow on, then harden off and plant out after frosts, 15–30cm (6–12in) apart.
**Feeding** Apply liquid feed weekly to beds or containers using a hand-held feeder.
**Problems** Damping off disease attacks seedlings. Use clean pots, fresh compost and treat with a copper-based fungicide if seedlings collapse.

## FLOWERING

**Season** Flowers appear on young plants before planting and then throughout summer. Take off dead flowers to keep new ones coming.
**Cutting** Not suitable as a cut flower.

## AFTER FLOWERING

**General** Remove when plants are past their best.

# IPOMOEA
*Morning glory*

*'HEAVENLY BLUE' morning glory never looks better than when scrambling through a host plant like this apple.*

## FEATURES

Look under ipomoea or morning glory in seed catalogues to find varieties of this stunning climber. Most familiar is sky-blue flowered 'Heavenly Blue'; others are red, pink, white, mauve, chocolate, one is striped, and 'Murasaki Jishi' is double-flowered. Average height is 3–4m (10–12ft). Plants will climb fences and other plants. For patios grow 3–4 plants in a 30cm (12in) pot up a wigwam of 1.5m (5ft) canes. A half-hardy annual with flowers mostly 7.5cm (3in) across. Seeds are poisonous.

### IPOMOEA AT A GLANCE

A half-hardy annual climber grown for its trumpet-shaped flowers which open in the morning. Frost hardy to 0°C (32°F).

| | | |
|---|---|---|
| JAN | / | |
| FEB | / | |
| MAR | / | |
| APR | sow | |
| MAY | grow on | |
| JUN | plant | |
| JULY | flowering | |
| AUG | flowering | |
| SEPT | flowering | |
| OCT | / | |
| NOV | / | |
| DEC | / | |

RECOMMENDED VARIETIES

Ipomoea hybrids:
 'Cardinal'
 'Chocolate'
 'Early Call Mixed'
 'Flying Saucers'
 'Grandpa Otts'
 'Heavenly Blue'
 'Mini Sky–Blue'
 'Murasaki Jishi'
 'Platycodon Flowered White'

## CONDITIONS

**Aspect** Must have full sun all day.
**Site** Mix rotted compost with soil before planting. In containers use multipurpose compost with slow-release fertiliser added. All ipomoeas must have shelter from wind, and must have support for their twining stems.

## GROWING METHOD

**Sowing** Soak the seeds in warm water the night before sowing, then sow one to a 9cm (3½in) pot, 2.5cm (1in) deep, in April. Keep in a temperature of at least 21°C (70°F) and put in bright light when the big pink seedlings come up 1–2 weeks later. Keep warm and grow on, potting on into 12.5cm (5in) pots when the roots fill the pot. Support shoots with short stakes. Gradually harden-off in late May, planting out or into containers in early June.
**Feeding** Feed monthly with a high-potash tomato food.
**Problems** Seedlings will turn yellow if they are kept too cold in the early stages. Red spider mite feeds on leaves – use a spray containing bifenthrin.

## FLOWERING

**Season** Summer.
**Cutting** Unsuitable for cutting.

## AFTER FLOWERING

**General** Use for composting when finished.

# KOCHIA
## *Summer cypress*

*SUMMER CYPRESS is so-called because it resembles a dwarf conifer in colour and shape. In early autumn plants turn bright red.*

*KOCHIA MAKES a bold plant for the focus of a bedding display – seen here with pink nicotianas and silver-leaved senecio.*

## FEATURES

Summer cypress is a bushy half-hardy foliage annual that grows up to 90cm (3ft) high with soft, light-green feathery foliage forming an upright cone- or dome-shape. 'Trichophylla' has narrow leaves and looks similar to a dwarf conifer in summer, turning to a fiery bronze red in autumn, hence its other common name of burning bush. Grow in groups of 2–3 or singly as the centrepiece of a bedding scheme.

### KOCHIA AT A GLANCE

A half-hardy annual grown for its light-green leaves on bushy plants which turn red in autumn. Frost hardy to 0°C (32°F).

| | | |
|---|---|---|
| JAN | / | |
| FEB | sow | |
| MAR | sow | |
| APR | grow on | |
| MAY | harden off/plant | |
| JUN | leaves | |
| JULY | leaves | |
| AUG | leaves | |
| SEPT | leaves | |
| OCT | leaves | |
| NOV | / | |
| DEC | / | |

RECOMMENDED VARIETIES

*Kochia scoparia:*
  'Trichophylla'

For all-green leaves
  'Evergreen'

## CONDITIONS

**Aspect**   Needs full sun to get the best leaf colour.
**Site**   Grows on most soils but must be well-drained. Add manure/compost before planting.

## GROWING METHOD

**Sowing**   Sow February/March on the surface of a 9cm (3½in) pot of moist multipurpose compost but do not cover. Keep at 16°C (61°F) in a bright spot, and expect seedlings in 2–3 weeks. When large enough, transplant to 9cm (3½in) pots of multipurpose compost and grow on, hardening off in late May and planting outdoors after the last frosts. Space plants at least 60cm (2ft) apart to allow room for development. They can also be planted in rows as a temporary and unusual summer 'hedge'.

**Feeding**   Water thoroughly in early summer for 2–3 weeks after planting. Extra feeding is not essential to get good results.

**Problems**   No particular problems.

## FLOWERING

**Season**   Not grown for flowers but leaves.
**Cutting**   Unsuitable for cutting.

## AFTER FLOWERING

**General**   Pull up and compost in autumn.

# LATHYRUS
## *Sweet pea*

*SWEET PEAS are perhaps the easiest and most rewarding of cut flowers you can grow. Choose a variety known for its fragrance.*

*CLIMBING VARIETIES of* Lathyrus odoratus *make useful 'living screens' in summer with the added benefits of colour and scent.*

## FEATURES

Varieties of *Lathyrus odoratus*, or sweet pea, occupy several pages in seed catalogues, but there are two basic groups – the tall climbers reaching 2–2.5m (6–8ft), used as cut flowers and for screening, and dwarf 'patio' varieties reaching up to 90cm (3ft) which are used in bedding, baskets and containers. Not all sweet peas have good scent, so check before buying seeds, and choose a fragrant mixed variety for a range of flower colours, which can be white, pink, red, mauve, orange or blue, as well as many with picotee and other patterns. Sweet peas are easily-grown hardy annuals.

## CONDITIONS

**Aspect**    Grow in full sun.

---

### LATHYRUS AT A GLANCE

A hardy annual climber producing often strongly-scented flowers which are ideal for cutting. Frost hardy to –15°C (5°F).

| | | |
|------|---------|---|
| JAN | / | |
| FEB | / | |
| MAR | sow | |
| APR | grow on | |
| MAY | plant | |
| JUN | flowering | |
| JULY | flowering | |
| AUG | flowering | |
| SEPT | flowering | |
| OCT | sow | |
| NOV | / | |
| DEC | / | |

RECOMMENDED VARIETIES

*Lathyrus odoratus:*
**Tall, fragrant varieties**
  'Bouquet Mixed'
  'Great Expectations'
  'Old Fashioned Mixed'
  'Old Spice Mixed'
**Dwarf/patio varieties**
  'Explorer'
  'Fantasia Mixed'
  'Jet-Set Mixed'
  'Knee-High'

---

**Site**    Needs well-drained soil packed with organic matter. Add compost or rotted manure the autumn before sowing or planting. Climbing varieties need canes, bean netting, fences or other supports to grow through. Use multipurpose compost for planting up baskets and patio containers.

## GROWING METHOD

**Sowing**    Seeds can be sown individually in 9cm (3½in) pots in February/March and germinated in a coldframe, cold porch, or even outdoors in a spot sheltered from rain. Nick or file the tough seed coat until a pale 'spot' appears, then sow 2.5cm (1in) deep in soil-based seed compost. Pinch out the growing tips when plants are 7.5cm (3in) tall to encourage sideshoots to grow. Grow outside, then plant out in May, 30cm (12in) apart for climbers, and 15–30cm (6–12in) apart for patio varieties used in baskets and containers.

**Feeding**    Plants benefit from a monthly feed with liquid tomato food. Water thoroughly in dry spells.

**Problems**    Mice will dig young seedlings up so set traps. Powdery mildew can attack leaves in the summer – use a spray containing sulphur.

## FLOWERING

**Season**    Seed can also be sown in October, and plants overwintered for flowers from early summer. Spring-sown plants flower from June.

**Cutting**    Cut when the first few flowers on the stalk are opening and stand up to their necks in water.

## AFTER FLOWERING

**General**    Cut off at ground level in autumn so the nitrogen-rich roots rot down in the soil.

# LAVATERA
*Annual mallow*

*'SILVER CUP' is one of the most popular varieties of annual mallow, with rose-pink flowers up to 12.5cm (5in) across.*

*IN MIXED BORDERS annual mallow can be sown direct into open patches of soil, for mounds of colour from mid to late summer.*

## FEATURES

White, rose, pink and red flowers with a silky sheen are characteristic of annual mallow. Plants grow between 60–120cm (2–4ft) depending on variety, and bloom continuously from mid-June onwards. Use them as the centrepiece in summer bedding schemes or grow in large blocks in annual borders. An easily-grown hardy annual that is also useful as a cut flower.

### LAVATERA AT A GLANCE

A hardy annual grown for its large, colourful summer flowers on bushy plants 60–120cm (2–4ft) tall. Frost hardy to –15°C (5°F).

| | | |
|---|---|---|
| JAN | / | |
| FEB | / | |
| MAR | sow | |
| APR | sow/thin out | |
| MAY | sow/thin out | |
| JUN | flowering | |
| JULY | flowering | |
| AUG | flowering | |
| SEPT | flowering | |
| OCT | / | |
| NOV | / | |
| DEC | / | |

RECOMMENDED VARIETIES

*Lavatera trimestris:*
 'Beauty Mixed'
 'Dwarf White Cherub'
 'Loveliness'
 'Mont Blanc'
 'Mont Rose'
 'Parade Mixed'
 'Pink Beauty'
 'Ruby Regis'
 'Silver Cup'

## CONDITIONS

**Aspect** Must have full sun all day.
**Site** Lavatera needs good drainage but not rich soil – plants flower better if the ground is hungry, making them good plants for light sandy soils. They do well in seaside gardens.

## GROWING METHOD

**Sowing** Seed is sown outdoors March–May, and earlier sowings mean earlier flowers. Mark out circles 60cm (2ft) or more across, then sow seed in short drills 1cm (½in) deep. Once seedlings appear thin them out gradually so they are 30–60cm (1–2ft) apart by early summer. Growing this way creates a roughly circular block of colour, which can be used as the centrepiece of a bedding scheme using annuals.
**Feeding** Feeding is not necessary. Water thoroughly in early summer during long dry spells.
**Problems** Sometimes killed suddenly by soil fungal diseases – grow in a new spot the next season.

## FLOWERING

**Season** Summer.
**Cutting** Grow a few plants just for cut stems.

## AFTER FLOWERING

**General** Leave a few plants to self-seed, then pull up.

# LIMNANTHES

*Poached egg flower*

*POACHED EGG FLOWER has 2.5cm (1in) wide flowers like tiny eggs in early summer, and attractive, divided, fern-like leaves.*

*THE SEEDS OF LIMNANTHES go everywhere after flowering and seem to enjoy spreading along path edges in particular.*

## FEATURES

*Limnanthes douglasii* has cup-shaped white flowers with bright yellow centres, which explains its common name of poached egg flower. Plants grow to 15–23cm (6–9in) in height and have a spreading habit. A hardy annual, it self-seeds very easily and keeps on coming. Grow in annual beds, along path edges and among other plants in borders.

### LIMNANTHES AT A GLANCE

A hardy annual which quickly self-seeds, producing masses of yellow/white flowers in summer. Frost hardy to –15°C (5°F).

| | | RECOMMENDED VARIETIES |
|---|---|---|
| JAN | / | *Limnanthes douglasii* |
| FEB | / | |
| MAR | sow | |
| APR | sow/thin | |
| MAY | sow/thin | |
| JUN | flowering | |
| JULY | flowering | |
| AUG | / | |
| SEPT | sow | |
| OCT | / | |
| NOV | / | |
| DEC | / | |

## CONDITIONS

**Aspect**  Prefers full sun and an open situation.
**Site**  Needs moisture-retentive soil with rotted organic matter mixed in well ahead of sowing.

## GROWING METHOD

**Sowing**  Spring or autumn are the sowing times. Sow from March to May or in September. Either sow seed in short drills 1cm (½in) deep or mark areas of soil, scatter the seed over the surface and rake in. Seedlings appear after 1–2 weeks and should be thinned out so they are about 7.5–15cm (3–6in) apart, although this is not too critical. If sowing in autumn do not thin until spring in case of winter losses.
**Feeding**  Feeding is not necessary, but water thoroughly in dry spells during early summer.
**Problems**  No special problems.

## FLOWERING

**Season**  Overwintered plants flower from late spring depending on the weather, and are very attractive to bees and beneficial garden insects.
**Cutting**  Not suitable for cutting.

## AFTER FLOWERING

**General**  Pull plants up as soon as they are over.

# LIMONIUM
*Statice*

*LONG AFTER the small pale flowers have faded the colourful papery bracts are still going strong, and they keep their colour when dried.*

*'PURPLE MONARCH' is a classic strain of statice for cutting and drying. It grows to 60cm (24in).*

## FEATURES

Annual varieties of *Limonium sinuatum* grow up to 90cm (3ft) tall and have peculiar winged stems. The actual flowers are small, but statice is grown for its papery bracts of purple, white, pink, apricot, yellow, rose or blue, which persist all summer, and can be used as a cut and dried flower. A half-hardy annual which is used solely for cutting, or in the case of the short varieties as a bedding/container plant.

## CONDITIONS

**Aspect**      Grow in full sun in an open position.

### LIMONIUM AT A GLANCE

A half-hardy annual grown for its heads of brightly coloured bracts used for bedding and drying. Frost hardy to –5°C (23°F).

| | | |
|---|---|---|
| JAN | / | RECOMMENDED VARIETIES |
| FEB | sow 🌱 | *Limonium sinuatum:* |
| MAR | sow/transplant 🌱 | **Tall varieties** |
| APR | grow on 🌱 | 'Art Shades Mixed' |
| MAY | grow on/harden 🌱 | 'Forever Mixed' |
| JUN | plant/grow 🌱 | 'Forever Moonlight' |
| JULY | flowering 🌸 | 'Sunburst Mixed' |
| AUG | flowers/cutting 🌸 | 'Sunset Mixed' |
| SEPT | flowers/cutting 🌸 | **Short varieties** |
| OCT | / | 'Biedermeier Mixed' |
| NOV | / | 'Petite Bouquet' |
| DEC | / | |

**Site**       Must have very well-drained soil, and is quite happy in sandy, light soils that are on the 'hungry' side. If growing dwarf varieties for containers use multipurpose compost. Statice does exceedingly well in seaside gardens.

## GROWING METHOD

**Sowing**     Sow seed in February/March in a 9cm (3½in) pot of multipurpose compost and keep at 18°C (64°F). Transplant to cell trays, grow on, then harden off in late May and plant after the last frosts 15–45cm (6–18in) apart. If growing for cut flowers, seed can be sown outdoors in rows from early May, 1cm (½in) deep and thinned to similar spacings.

**Feeding**    Does not need regular feeding, but water well if dry straight after planting out.

**Problems**   Plants may rot on heavy, wet soils, and powdery mildew can attack the leaves in late summer, but this is rarely serious.

## FLOWERING

**Season**     Long flowering period throughout summer.

**Cutting**    Ideal cut flower. Can be used fresh, or cut and dried by hanging bunches upside down in a dry airy place. Cut when the flowerheads are showing maximum colour. Dried flowers retain their colour well over a long period.

## AFTER FLOWERING

**General**    Pull plants up and compost once all the flowers have been cut or have gone over.

# LINARIA
## *Toadflax*

*WHEN SOWN IN BOLD PATCHES varieties of* Linaria maroccana *soon knit together to produce a tapestry of colour if one of the mixtures such as 'Fairy Bouquet' is grown. Clumps can also be carefully lifted and planted into patio pots in late spring and early summer.*

## FEATURES

Linaria is commonly known as toadflax and has dainty little flowers like tiny snapdragons in a wide colour range including white, cream, yellow, red, blue and pink. Plants grow 23–60cm (9–24in) and are good massed in drifts in annual borders, or used as fillers in mixed border plantings. Most annual toadflax are varieties of *Linaria maroccana*. A hardy annual that can be sown direct outdoors.

### LINARIA AT A GLANCE

A hardy annual grown for its spikes of pretty flowers like small snapdragons appearing in summer. Frost hardy to −15°C (5°F).

| | | |
|---|---|---|
| JAN | / | RECOMMENDED VARIETIES |
| FEB | / | |
| MAR | sow | *Linaria anticaria* |
| APR | sow/thin out | |
| MAY | sow/thin out | *Linaria maroccana:* |
| JUN | thin/flowers |   'Fairy Bouquet' |
| JULY | flowering |   'Fantasia Blue' |
| AUG | flowering |   'Fantasia Mixed' |
| SEPT | flowering |   'Fantasia Pink' |
| OCT | / |   'Northern Lights' |
| NOV | / | |
| DEC | / | *Linaria reticulata:* |
| | |   'Crown Jewels' |

## CONDITIONS

**Aspect**    Needs a warm, sunny spot.
**Site**    Well-drained soil enriched with manure or compost ahead of planting is essential. Very good plants can be grown on light, sandy soils.

## GROWING METHOD

**Sowing**    Seeds are best sown in short drills 1cm (½in) deep March–May. Mark the sowing areas with a ring of light-coloured sand and label if sowing more than one annual in the same bed. The seedlings will appear in rows and can be told from nearby weed seedlings quite easily. Thin the seedlings out so they are finally 10–15cm (4–6in) apart by early summer. Alternatively, leave them to grow as small clumps of 4–6 plants every 30cm (12in) or so.
**Feeding**    Feeding is rarely needed but water well after the final thinning if the soil is dry.
**Problems**    No special problems.

## FLOWERING

**Season**    Flowers appear early to mid summer.
**Cutting**    Not usually used for cutting.

## AFTER FLOWERING

**General**    Leave a few plants to die down and self-seed. Others can be pulled up and composted.

# LOBELIA
## *Lobelia*

*LOBELIA FLOWERS are tubular with a large lower 'lip' divided into three rounded lobes. Dark flowers have pale throats.*

*IN THIS HANGING BASKET lobelias mingle with begonias and brachyscome, and bright red nasturtiums creep up from below.*

## FEATURES

Choose the bushier 'edging' varieties for bedding schemes and the 'trailers' for hanging baskets, flower bags and containers. Flower colour ranges from white through pink, mauve and white to blue, and striking two-toned varieties like 'Riviera Blue Splash' are also available. Edgers grow 10–15cm (4–6in) tall, trailers up to 45cm (18in) long when well fed, and plants have a similar spread. Varieties of *Lobelia erinus* are available as single or mixed colours, and modern coated seed makes sowing much easier. A range of varieties are available as young plants by mail order. Half-hardy.

### LOBELIA AT A GLANCE

A half-hardy annual used as an edging plant or a trailing plant for baskets, with many small flowers. Frost hardy to 0°C (32°F).

| | | |
|---|---|---|
| JAN | sow | |
| FEB | sow/transplant | |
| MAR | sow/transplant | |
| APR | grow on | |
| MAY | harden off/plant | |
| JUN | flowering | |
| JULY | flowering | |
| AUG | flowering | |
| SEPT | flowering | |
| OCT | / | |
| NOV | / | |
| DEC | / | |

**RECOMMENDED VARIETIES**

*Lobelia erinus:*

**Edging varieties**
  'Cambridge Blue'
  'Crystal Palace'
  'Mrs Clibran Improved'
  'Riviera Lilac'

**Trailing varieties**
  'Cascade Mixed'
  'Fountains Mixed'
  'Regatta Mixed'
  'String of Pearls Mixed'

## CONDITIONS

**Aspect**   Flowers best when grown in full sun.

**Site**   Enrich soil with rotted compost or manure before planting. Drainage must be good, but lobelia must also have adequate moisture all through the season. For baskets and containers use multipurpose compost and add slow-release fertiliser granules before planting up.

## GROWING METHOD

**Sowing**   Sow January–March in a 9cm (3½in) pot of multipurpose compost. Sow the tiny seeds evenly over the surface but do not cover, and put in a well-lit spot at 18°C (64°F). When the seedlings form a green 'mat', carefully tease them apart into small clumps of 4–6, and transplant each clump to one unit of a multi-cell tray. Grow on, harden off in late May and plant after frosts.

**Feeding**   Feed fortnightly with high-potash liquid feed, and never allow the plants to dry out.

**Problems**   Trouble-free, but if seedlings keel over in spring water with copper-based fungicide.

## FLOWERING

**Season**   Flowers appear from June onwards.

**Cutting**   Not suitable for cutting.

## AFTER FLOWERING

**General**   Go over plants with shears when they look untidy and water with liquid feed – this encourages more flowers. Compost in autumn.

# LOBULARIA
## *Alyssum*

ALYSSUM IS COMPACT *and this makes it the ideal edging plant to fill in between other summer bedders. Flowers smell of honey.*

'CARPET OF SNOW' *is used here in a bed to create living lines and patterns around slightly taller plants such as these violas.*

## FEATURES

*Lobularia maritima*, alyssum, has masses of tiny flowers in various colours in round heads; white, pink, lavender and purple. All varieties smell sweetly of honey, although you need to get up close. None grow more than 15cm (6in) high, making alyssum ideal as an edging plant, but it is also useful for planting in pots, troughs and hanging baskets.

## CONDITIONS

**Aspect**     Grow alyssum in a spot receiving full sun.

### LOBULARIA AT A GLANCE

A low-growing hardy annual for edging summer bedding schemes, with honey-scented flowers. Frost hardy to –15°C (5°F).

| | | |
|---|---|---|
| JAN | / | **RECOMMENDED VARIETIES** |
| FEB | sow | *Lobularia maritima :* |
| MAR | sow/transplant | 'Aphrodite' |
| APR | sow/grow on | 'Creamery' |
| MAY | sow/harden off | 'Easter Basket Mixed' |
| JUN | flowering | 'Easter Bonnet' |
| JULY | flowering | 'Golf Mixed' |
| AUG | flowering | 'Golf Rose' |
| SEPT | flowering | 'Little Dorrit' |
| OCT | / | 'Rosie O'Day' |
| NOV | / | 'Snow Carpet' |
| DEC | / | 'Snow Crystals' |

**Site**     Must have well-drained soil and adding rotted organic matter helps retain soil moisture. For baskets and patio containers plant using multipurpose potting compost.

## GROWING METHOD

**Sowing**     Alyssum grown for bedding and containers is best raised in early spring. Sow a whole packet of seeds in February/March in a 9cm (3½in) pot of multipurpose compost, and just cover. When seedlings are 1cm (½in) tall split up into small clumps of 4–6 seedlings and transplant each to individual units of a multi-cell tray. This is especially useful to get a good spread of different flowers colours when growing a mixed variety. Grow on and harden off in late May before planting out. Seeds can also be sown direct into the soil in an annual border during April/May 1cm (½in) deep.

**Feeding**     Extra feeding is unnecessary.

**Problems**     Look out for slugs which will attack newly-planted alyssum, especially after rain.

## FLOWERING

**Season**     Flowers often appear before planting and until late summer – clip them over with shears and water well to encourage a second flush.

**Cutting**     Not suitable as a cut flower.

## AFTER FLOWERING

**General**     Seeds will self-sow very easily, and come up the following spring. Compost when finished.

# LUNARIA
## *Honesty*

THE SEEDHEADS *of* Lunaria annua *are sought after for dried flower arrangements. Here they are still in the green stages of growth.*

*'ALBA VARIEGATA' has leaves splashed with creamy-white and also white flowers. It adds easy and quick colour to spring borders.*

## FEATURES

Honesty, *Lunaria annua*, a hardy biennial is also known as the money plant because of its large circular, smooth, silvery seedheads that resemble coins. It grows up to 90cm (3ft) tall and is a plant that is best left to do its own thing, self-seeding very quickly, and thriving under dry hedges where most plants will not grow, and will seed into mixed borders. Flowers are purple or white and appear in early spring, and variegated varieties are available.

### LUNARIA AT A GLANCE

A hardy biennial grown for its pretty purple/white flowers followed by large silvery seedheads. Frost hardy to −15°C (5°F).

| | | RECOMMENDED VARIETIES |
|---|---|---|
| JAN | / | *Lunaria annua:* |
| FEB | / | 'Fine Mixed' |
| MAR | sow/flowers | 'Mixed' |
| APR | thin/flowers | |
| MAY | thin/flowers | |
| JUN | flowering | **Variegated leaves** |
| JULY | / | 'Variegata' |
| AUG | / | |
| SEPT | / | **White flowers** |
| OCT | / | 'Alba Variegata' |
| NOV | / | |
| DEC | / | |

## CONDITIONS

**Aspect** Succeeds in sun or the shade cast by hedges and large shrubs.

**Site** Thriving in poor soils, plants grow larger still if they are sown into soil that has been improved with rotted manure or compost, and produce the best seedheads for drying.

## GROWING METHOD

**Sowing** Mark out patches using sand and sow the large seeds 2.5cm (1in) deep in short drills, with 5–7.5cm (2–3in) between each seed in March. Seedlings are quick to appear and can be thinned or left to develop as they are. Next spring look out for seedlings and move them when small to where you want plants to grow.

**Feeding** Needs no extra feeding or watering.

## FLOWERING

**Season** Flowers from early spring to early summer.

**Cutting** Can be cut for flowers but some must be left to set seed if you want the large, silvery heads.

## AFTER FLOWERING

**General** Cut when the seedheads are mature and dry, on a warm day, and hang upside-down in a dry, airy place until you can carefully remove the outer skin of the pod. Leave a few plants to die down naturally and self-seed.

# LUPINUS
## *Annual lupin*

*SHORTER AND SQUATTER than their perennial cousins, annual lupins can create a sea of colour when sown in large drifts like this. As the flowers fade the spikes should be removed completely with secateurs to divert energy into new flowers rather than seed pods.*

## FEATURES

By growing annual lupins from seed you can enjoy the features of their perennial relatives without giving up too much space in the garden. Annual lupins are smaller, growing between 30–90cm (1–3ft) tall, but have very colourful spikes in mixed shades and also striking single colours such as the blue-flowered *Lupinus texensis*. Hardy annuals. Seeds and plants are poisonous if eaten.

### LUPINUS AT A GLANCE

A hardy annual grown for its spikes of colourful and spicey-scented flowers during summer. Frost hardy to –15°C (5°F).

| | | RECOMMENDED VARIETIES |
|---|---|---|
| JAN | / | **Lupinus hybrids:** |
| FEB | / | 'Biancaneve' |
| MAR | / | 'New White' |
| APR | sow | 'Pink Javelin' |
| MAY | thin out | 'Pixie Delight' |
| JUN | flowering | 'Sunrise' |
| JULY | flowering | **Yellow flowers** |
| AUG | flowering | *Lupinus luteus* |
| SEPT | flowering | **Blue flowers** |
| OCT | / | *Lupinus texensis* |
| NOV | / | *Lupinus varius* |
| DEC | / | |

## CONDITIONS

**Aspect**  Needs full sun.
**Site**  Well-drained, light soil is best for annual lupins, but mix in rotted manure or compost.

## GROWING METHOD

**Sowing**  The large seeds can go straight into the ground in April, but to ensure germination the tough seed coat must be nicked with a sharp knife or rubbed down with a file until the pale inside just shows. Next, soak the seeds on wet tissue paper and sow when they have swollen up, 7.5–15cm (3–6in) apart and 5cm (2in) deep, where you want plants to grow. Thin seedlings to 15cm (6in) apart when well established. To grow in pots do the same, sowing one seed to a 9cm (3½in) pot, then plant out.
**Feeding**  Lupins need no extra feeding.
**Problems**  Fat green lupin aphids can kill entire plants, so use a spray containing permethrin.

## FLOWERING

**Season**  Flowers appear from midsummer.
**Cutting**  Cut when some buds at the base of the flower spike are fully open.

## AFTER FLOWERING

**General**  Cut off to leave the nitrogen-rich roots to rot in the ground, and compost the tops.

# MALCOLMIA
### *Virginian stock*

*PINK IS JUST one of the colours found in Virginian stocks. Expect reds, yellows and whites from a variety like 'Fine Mixed'.*

*JUST FOUR WEEKS after sowing plants will be in flower. Malcolmia maritima thrives in the thin light soils of seaside gardens.*

## FEATURES

Keep a packet of Virginian stock, *Malcolmia maritima* seed to hand at all times and sow a pinch of seeds every two weeks in gaps and under windows – plants will flower just a month later. They grow 15–20cm (6–8in) high with small, single, four-petalled, sweetly scented flowers in red, mauve, pink, yellow and white from June–September. They can also be sown into patio tubs. Hardy annual.

### MALCOLMIA AT A GLANCE

Hardy annual grown for its pink, red, yellow or white flowers. Flowers a month after sowing. Frost hardy to –15°C (5°F).

| | | |
|---|---|---|
| JAN | / | |
| FEB | / | |
| MAR | sow | |
| APR | sow/flowers | |
| MAY | sow/flowers | |
| JUN | sow/flowers | |
| JULY | sow/flowers | |
| AUG | sow/flowers | |
| SEPT | sow/flowers | |
| OCT | sow | |
| NOV | / | |
| DEC | / | |

RECOMMENDED VARIETIES

*Malcolmia maritima:*
  'Fine Mixed'
  'Mixed'

## CONDITIONS

**Aspect** Prefers full sun but tolerates some shade.
**Site** Will grow on most soils but needs good drainage to do well.

## GROWING METHOD

**Sowing** Seed can literally be scattered in small patches 30cm (12in) across on the soil where you want flowers and mixed in using your fingertips, or it is simply scattered along the cracks in paths and driveways, from March onwards, and repeated every few weeks all through the summer. Mark sown areas in borders with a label or circle of light-coloured sand. Seedlings soon come up and there is no need to bother with thinning. For early flowers the following spring sow in October.
**Feeding** Not necessary.
**Problems** Trouble-free.

## FLOWERING

**Season** Expect flowers all summer long with repeat sowings.
**Cutting** Unsuitable as a cut flower.

## AFTER FLOWERING

**General** Pull up as soon as the plants are over, and resow. Self-sown seedlings soon appear.

# MATTHIOLA
*Brompton stock*

*WHEN BEDDED-OUT in spring Brompton stocks provide an early splash of colour and fill the air with scent on warm days.*

*FLOWER COLOUR varies, and it should be possible to see the colour in the flower buds before you plant, ensuring an even display.*

## FEATURES

The sweetly scented flowers of Brompton stocks are held above the grey-green leaves on plants up to 45cm (18in) tall. There is a full range of pastel colours with some stronger purples, crimson and magenta as well; the flowers are double. Derived from *Matthiola incana*, Brompton stocks are lovely in massed spring plantings, giving off a delicious strong fragrance. They are grown as biennials.

## CONDITIONS

**Aspect**  Need full sun and a sheltered position.
**Site**  Must have well-drained soil. Incorporate rotted manure or compost into the soil a few weeks before planting. Tall varieties will need short stakes to prevent their flowers flopping.

### MATTHIOLA AT A GLANCE

A hardy biennial sown in summer for strongly-scented pink flowers the following spring. Frost hardy to −15°C (5°F).

| | | RECOMMENDED VARIETIES |
|---|---|---|
| JAN | grow on 🌱 | *Matthiola incana:* |
| FEB | plant 🌱 | 'Brompton Mixed' |
| MAR | plant 🌱 | 'Brompton Dwarf Mixed' |
| APR | flowering 🌸 | 'Spring Flowering Mixed' |
| MAY | flowering 🌸 | |
| JUN | sow 🌰 | |
| JULY | sow/transplant 🌰 | |
| AUG | transplant 🌱 | |
| SEPT | grow on 🌱 | |
| OCT | grow on 🌱 | |
| NOV | grow on 🌱 | |
| DEC | grow on 🌱 | |

## GROWING METHOD

**Sowing**  June/July is the time to sow seed, in a 9cm (3½in) pot of multipurpose compost. When the seedlings are large enough, transplant one seedling to a 9cm (3½in) pot of multipurpose compost, water well and grow on. Later, pot on into 12.5cm (5in) pots. When the first frosts arrive take the young plants into a coldframe, cold greenhouse or porch, standing them outside during mild spells all through the winter months. Keep on the dry side and only water when they wilt. Plant out from February onwards when the soil is workable, or pot on into large pots and grow in a cool conservatory or porch with canes for support.
**Feeding**  Do not feed until 2–3 weeks before planting out, then give a general purpose liquid feed.
**Problems**  Cabbage butterflies will lay eggs on the young plants in late summer and the caterpillars can strip leaves, so use a spray containing permethrin, or pick them off by hand.

## FLOWERING

**Season**  Brompton stocks will fill beds and borders with colour and scent during April and May, weather permitting. They perform best in calm, mild spells with plenty of sunshine. While most plants will have double flowers, there may be singles which can be put to one side, planted separately, and used for cutting.
**Cutting**  A good cut flower. Scald stems after picking and change vase water every couple of days.

## AFTER FLOWERING

**General**  Dig plants up when the show is over and prepare the ground for summer bedding plants. Add to the compost heap/bin.

# MIMULUS
## *Monkey flower*

MONKEY FLOWERS *have blooms which are face-like and marked with intricate patterns and spotting. They are good for shade.*

PLANT MIMULUS *along the edges of a path. Monkey flowers will bloom in just nine weeks.*

## FEATURES

Mimulus or monkey flower is grown as a half-hardy annual and is useful for summer bedding and containers, with bright flowers in a range of colours, mainly red and orange, on plants 30–45cm (12–18in) tall and wide. It is very useful for growing in shaded and wet spots.

## CONDITIONS

**Aspect**   Will grow in sun or shade.

### MIMULUS AT A GLANCE

Grown as a half-hardy annual for bedding, windowboxes and hanging baskets. Colourful flowers. Frost hardy to –15°C (5°F).

| | | |
|---|---|---|
| JAN | / | |
| FEB | sow | |
| MAR | sow/transplant | |
| APR | grow on | |
| MAY | grow on/harden | |
| JUN | flowering | |
| JULY | flowering | |
| AUG | flowering | |
| SEPT | flowering | |
| OCT | / | |
| NOV | / | |
| DEC | / | |

RECOMMENDED VARIETIES

Mimulus hybrids:
'Calypso'
'Extra Choice Mixed'
'Magic Ivory'
'Magic Pastels Mixed'
'Malibu'
'Malibu Orange'
'Malibu Sunshine'
'Queen's Prize Mixed'
'Sparkles'
'Viva'

**Site**   Needs moist soil so dig in plenty of rotted organic matter well ahead of planting. Use a peat- or coir-based multipurpose compost for growing mimulus in containers. Add slow-release fertiliser granules when planting.

## GROWING METHOD

**Sowing**   Sow in 9cm (3½in) pots in February/March, barely covering the fine seed. Keep at 12°C (54°F) in bright light and expect seedlings after about two weeks. When large enough transplant to cell trays and grow on until the end of May, then harden off and plant from mid-May onwards, 15–30cm (6–12in) apart, or in groups of 2–3 in troughs and pots.

**Feeding**   Feed monthly with liquid feed and ensure that containers never dry out or flowering will be reduced and plants damaged.

**Problems**   If slugs attack plants growing in shaded areas protect with slug pellets or scatter sharp grit to make a physical barrier. Container-grown plants suffer in excessive heat so move them to a position where they are out of midday sun.

## FLOWERING

**Season**   Summer, from June onwards.
**Cutting**   Not suitable for cutting.

## AFTER FLOWERING

**General**   Pull up and compost when finished.

# MOLUCCELLA
## *Bells of Ireland*

THE FLOWERS OF Moluccella laevis *are actually small, pale, and found in the centre of each of the showier bell-like bracts.*

*MOLUCCELLA is ideal for use in mixed borders to add a welcome touch of vivid green. Sow in patches 60cm (2ft) across.*

## FEATURES

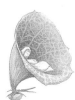

A half-hardy annual, also known as shell flower, moluccella is very lightly scented, and produces 60–90cm (2–3ft) tall spikes in summer. It has small flowers surrounded by the more obvious and showy bell- or shell-like apple-green bracts. You can grow moluccella in flower beds and mixed borders, but its main value is as a cut flower, either fresh or dried. It is long-lasting when dried in late summer, the green spikes gradually fade from green to pale brown through autumn and into winter.

## CONDITIONS

**Aspect**  Needs an open spot in full sun.

### MOLUCCELLA AT A GLANCE

A half-hardy annual grown for its tall spikes of green bracts which are used for drying. Frost hardy to 0°C (32°F).

| | | RECOMMENDED VARIETIES |
|---|---|---|
| JAN | / | |
| FEB | sow | *Moluccella laevis* |
| MAR | sow | |
| APR | transplant/grow | |
| MAY | plant/sow | |
| JUN | flowering | |
| JULY | flowering | |
| AUG | flowering | |
| SEPT | flowers/cutting | |
| OCT | / | |
| NOV | / | |
| DEC | / | |

**Site**  Must have good drainage, and working rotted manure or compost into the ground before sowing or planting helps. Avoid exposed, windy spots or the tall stems may be flattened.

## GROWING METHOD

**Sowing**  Either sow seed in 9cm (3½in) pots of multipurpose compost in February/March at 18°C (64°F), or sow directly in the soil where they are to grow in late April and May. Gradually thin out so plants are spaced 30–40cm (12–16in) apart. Plants raised under cover are hardened off before being planted.

**Feeding**  If organic matter has already been added to the soil, extra feeding is not necessary, but keep plants well watered during long dry spells.

**Problems**  Seeds can sometimes be slow and difficult to germinate, so put them in the bottom of a refrigerator for two weeks before you sow, to 'chill' them, then sow in pots as described above and expect seedlings in 2–3 weeks.

## FLOWERING

**Season**  Even after the actual flowers have faded the green bracts go on providing colour and interest until they are cut for drying.

**Cutting**  Ideal as a cut flower, used fresh or dried. Cut when flowers are well formed. Leaves can be removed to display the green bracts better. The stems dry to a light brown colour.

## AFTER FLOWERING

**General**  Remove roots once stems have been harvested, but leave a few behind to develop on the plant and finally shed seeds, which will self-sow.

# MYOSOTIS

*Forget-me-not*

*FORGET-ME-NOTS flower from early spring after growing slowly during the winter months. Flowers often have yellow 'eyes'.*

*'MONTE CARLO' early double tulips rising up through a haze of forget-me-nots is a springtime classic that is seldom bettered.*

## FEATURES

Forget-me-nots are useful spring bedding plants, producing swathes of pink, blue or white flowers from April onwards. They go well with bulbs like tulips which push up through the myosotis flowers. Grow as a hardy biennial and use shorter varieties such as 'Blue Ball', reaching 15cm (6in), in winter and spring patio containers. None grow more than 30cm (12in) tall, and these are the ideal choice for spring bedding displays. Available by mail order in autumn as ready-grown young plants.

### MYOSOTIS AT A GLANCE

A hardy biennial grown for its small flowers which appear in masses from early spring. Frost hardy to −15°C (5°F).

| | | RECOMMENDED VARIETIES |
|---|---|---|
| JAN | / | *Myosotis sylvatica:* |
| FEB | / | 'Blue Ball' |
| MAR | / | 'Carmine King' |
| APR | flowering | 'Compindi' |
| MAY | flowers/sow | 'Indigo' |
| JUN | sow | 'Light Blue' |
| JULY | grow on | 'Music' |
| AUG | grow on | 'Rosylva' |
| SEPT | grow on | 'Royal Blue' |
| OCT | plant | 'Spring Symphony Mxd' |
| NOV | / | 'Victoria Mixed' |
| DEC | / | |

## CONDITIONS

**Aspect**   Full or dappled sunlight is suitable.

**Site**   Responds well to soil with plenty of rotted compost or manure mixed in that holds plenty of moisture. When planting containers in autumn ensure good drainage and use a multipurpose compost.

## GROWING METHOD

**Sowing**   Seed is sown direct into the ground May–July, in drills 1cm (½in) deep. Thin seedlings as they develop so plants are eventually 7.5–15cm (3–6in) apart, keep weed free and water copiously in dry spells. Plant into their flowering positions/containers in October and water to settle in.

**Feeding**   Do not feed after planting in autumn, but scatter a general granular fertiliser around plants in spring as they show signs of growth.

**Problems**   Powdery mildew can affect leaves but this is generally not worth treating.

## FLOWERING

**Season**   From late winter to early summer.

**Cutting**   Not suitable for cutting.

## AFTER FLOWERING

**General**   Remove plants to make way for summer bedding, but if you leave a few to die down they will self-sow into the soil.

# NEMESIA
*Nemesia*

*THE TWO-LIPPED FLOWERS of nemesias come in an array of colours and they all have patterns deep in the flower's 'throat'.*

*NEMESIAS CARRY THEIR flowers in large, almost flattish heads with individual flowers pointing off in all directions.*

## FEATURES

No varieties of *Nemesia strumosa* grow more than 30cm (12in) high making them ideal for beds and containers. Grown as a half-hardy annual, flowers can be single colours or bright and varied mixtures. Good as edging for troughs and windowboxes. Very easy to grow.

## CONDITIONS

**Aspect**   Must have full sun to grow successfully.

### NEMESIA AT A GLANCE

A half-hardy annual grown for its pretty lipped flowers, used for bedding and patio containers. Frost hardy to 0°C (32°F).

| | | | |
|---|---|---|---|
| JAN | / | RECOMMENDED VARIETIES | |
| FEB | / | *Nemesia strumosa:* | |
| MAR | sow | **Mixed colours** | |
| APR | sow/transplant | 'Carnival Mixed' | |
| MAY | harden off/plant | 'Pastel Mixed' | |
| JUN | flowering | 'Sparklers' | |
| JULY | flowering | 'Tapestry' | |
| AUG | flowering | **Single colours** | |
| SEPT | flowering | 'Blue Gem' | |
| OCT | / | 'Fire King' | |
| NOV | / | 'KLM' | |
| DEC | / | 'National Ensign' | |

**Site**   In containers use multipurpose compost with slow-release fertiliser mixed well in. Soil with plenty of organic matter dug in well ahead of planting gives good results, and must be well-drained.

## GROWING METHOD

**Sowing**   Raise plants by sowing in small pots of soil-based seed compost starting in March/April (and repeating every few weeks for a succession of flowers), just covering the seeds. Keep at 15°C (60°F) in a light place, and transplant to cell trays when seedlings are large enough to handle. Grow on and harden off in late May before planting after the last frosts, 15–30cm (6–12in) apart. In containers make sure they are not swamped.

**Feeding**   Give a liquid feed to plants grown as bedding every two weeks, with a hand-held feeder. Regular watering in dry spells is vital.

**Problems**   Plants may rot off in heavy, wet soils.

## FLOWERING

**Season**   For more flowerheads, pinch out growing tips of plants when they are 10cm (4in) high.

**Cutting**   Not suited to cutting.

## AFTER FLOWERING

**General**   Pull plants up when finished – this is quite often as they have a short flowering period.

# NEMOPHILA
*Baby blue eyes*

*NEMOPHILA MENZIESII flowers are a brilliant sky-blue with a distinctive paler 'eye', carried over bright green feathery leaves.*

*NEMOPHILA can be grown with other hardy annuals such as limnanthes, the poached egg flower, for a striking colour combination.*

## FEATURES

Nemophila is an easy annual sown in autumn or spring. Flowers are sky-blue, white, or black/white. Plants grow to 20cm (8in) high, with feathery leaves and a carpeting habit. Use them in borders, on rockeries and around the edge of containers and windowboxes.

## CONDITIONS

**Aspect**   Needs full sun or part shade to succeed.

### NEMOPHILA AT A GLANCE

A hardy spreading annual grown for its flowers for beds, rockeries and container edges. Frost hardy to −15°C (5°F).

| | | RECOMMENDED VARIETIES |
|---|---|---|
| JAN | / | *Nemophila menziesii:* |
| FEB | / | (Also listed as *N.insignis*) |
| MAR | / | 'Baby Blue Eyes' |
| APR | sow | 'Penny Black' |
| MAY | flowers/sow | 'Snowstorm' |
| JUN | flowering | |
| JULY | flowering | *Nemophila maculata:* |
| AUG | flowering | 'Five Spot' |
| SEPT | flowers/sow | |
| OCT | / | |
| NOV | / | |
| DEC | / | |

**Site**   Needs well-drained soil, but mix in well-rotted organic matter before sowing to retain moisture. Nemophila will thrive in most multipurpose composts used in containers.

## GROWING METHOD

**Sowing**   Sow seeds straight into the soil in autumn or spring, in drills 1cm (½in) deep. Seeds sown in autumn will produce young plants which survive the winter and flower earlier. Gradually thin plants out so they are 7.5–15cm (3–6in) apart as flowers appear.

**Feeding**   On well-prepared soil feeding is unnecessary, although large beds can be fed monthly with a general liquid feed applied through a hand-held feeder. Keep plants watered in dry spells or they may quickly die off.

**Problems**   Aphids can attack the soft leaves, so use a spray containing permethrin.

## FLOWERING

**Season**   On autumn-sown plants flowers appear from early spring to the first frosts, but appear slightly later on spring-sown plants.

**Cutting**   Not suitable for use as a cut flower.

## AFTER FLOWERING

**General**   Leave plants to set seed and die back before removing – nemophila self-seeds and plants will appear on their own each spring.

# NICOTIANA
### *Tobacco plant*

*'DOMINO SALMON PINK' is a popular variety of nicotiana because of its striking colour and sheer flower power. Here in a bedding display it covers the ground and produces tubular, salmon-pink flowers non-stop through the summer. It is also useful for containers.*

## FEATURES

Not grown for tobacco but for their tubular flowers. Choose from dwarf modern varieties growing 30cm (1ft) tall with upward-facing flowers, for bedding and containers, to *Nicotiana sylvestris* at 1.5m (5ft) for large borders – plant it behind other plants and especially against a dark evergreen background so that the large leaves as well as the flowers are shown off to best effect. Some release scent in the evening, so plant near doors and windows, or grow a few in large tubs that can be moved into the house or conservatory on a warm summer evening. Flowers can be pink to lime-green. A half-hardy annual. Widely available as young plants in a good selection of varieties.

### NICOTIANA AT A GLANCE

A half-hardy annual grown for it colourful and often scented flowers, used in bedding/containers. Frost hardy to 0°C (32°F).

| | | |
|---|---|---|
| JAN | / | |
| FEB | / | |
| MAR | sow | |
| APR | transplant/grow on | |
| MAY | harden off/plant | |
| JUN | flowering | |
| JULY | flowering | |
| AUG | flowering | |
| SEPT | flowering | |
| OCT | / | |
| NOV | / | |
| DEC | / | |

RECOMMENDED VARIETIES

*Nicotiana sanderae:*
  'Domino Mixed'
  'Domino Salmon Pink'
  'Havana Appleblossom'
  'Hippy Mixed'
  'Lime Green'
  'Merlin Peach'

*Nicotiana langsdorfii*

*Nicotiana sylvestris*

## CONDITIONS

**Aspect**  Full sun or light shade. The flowers stay open longer in sun.

**Site**  Grow in well-drained, moisture retentive soil with rotted manure/compost mixed in. For container growing use multipurpose compost.

## GROWING METHOD

**Sowing**  Use 9cm (3½in) diameter pots of multipurpose compost, sow the fine seed on the surface in March, but do not cover, and keep in a light place at 21°C (70°F). Tiny seedlings emerge within three weeks. Transplant to cell trays of multipurpose compost or into 9cm (3½in) diameter pots when each young plant has developed 3–4 small leaves. Grow on and harden off in late May, then plant after the last frosts in your area, 30–45cm (12–18in) apart depending on the variety grown.

**Feeding**  Liquid feed weekly outdoors. Add slow-release fertiliser granules to container compost before planting.

**Problems**  Use a spray containing pirimicarb for aphids. Destroy plants attacked by virus, showing any puckered and mottled leaves

## FLOWERING

**Season**  Flowers all summer. Nip off dead flowers.

**Cutting**  Not suitable.

## AFTER FLOWERING

**General**  Remove plants after first frosts. It is possible to collect seed from *Nicotiana sylvestris* which can then be sown the following spring.

# NIGELLA
*Love-in-a-mist*

*'MISS JEKYLL' with semi-double blue flowers is a reliable variety of* Nigella damascena. *Each flower has a feathery 'collar'.*

*AFTER THE FLOWERS come the curiously attractive seedheads that give the plant its other common name, devil-in-a-bush.*

## FEATURES

Love-in-a-mist has fine, feathery leaves, with a fringe of foliage surrounding and slightly veiling each of the flowers, hence its common name. When the spiky seed pods appear it is also called devil-in-a-bush. Flowers are blue, pale and deep pink, white or purple. Nigella grows 45cm (18in) tall and is good for big drifts in beds or for cutting. Hardy annual. The variety 'Transformer' has novel seed pods.

## CONDITIONS

**Aspect**    Give it a sunny spot in an open position.

### NIGELLA AT A GLANCE

A hardy annual grown for its flowers and its attractive, inflated seed pods which can be dried. Frost hardy to −15°C (5°F).

| | | RECOMMENDED VARIETIES |
|---|---|---|
| JAN | / | *Nigella damascena:* |
| FEB | / |   'Dwarf Moody Blue' |
| MAR | sow |   'Miss Jekyll' |
| APR | flowers/thin |   'Miss Jekyll Alba' |
| MAY | flowering |   'Mulberry Rose' |
| JUN | flowering |   'Oxford Blue' |
| JULY | flowering |   'Persian Jewels' |
| AUG | flowering |   'Shorty Blue' |
| SEPT | flowers/sow | |
| OCT | / | *Nigella orientalis:* |
| NOV | / |   'Transformer' |
| DEC | / | |

## Site

Needs good drainage but isn't too fussy about soils – rotted organic matter may be dug in ahead of planting, but this is not essential, and good results can be had on quite thin, poor soils as long as it is grown in full sun.

## GROWING METHOD

**Sowing**    Sow in March or September, in short drills 1cm (½in) deep. Thin plants as they grow so there is about 15–20cm (6–8in) between them as they begin to produce flower buds. Leave thinning of autumn-sown plants until spring in case there are winter losses. Plants can also be raised in cell trays, sowing 2–3 seeds per tray and removing all but the strongest seedling – nigella does not like disturbance.

**Feeding**    Does not need extra feeding during summer.

**Problems**    Plants are trouble free.

## FLOWERING

**Season**    Autumn-sown plants flower from late spring, spring-sown from early summer.

**Cutting**    Delightful cut flower. Remove foliage from lower part of stalk to prolong flower life.

## AFTER FLOWERING

**General**    The inflated seed pods that form are useful in dried flower arrangements. Pick stems after pods have dried on the plant and hang upside down in a warm, airy place. Nigella self-seeds prolifically and will produce masses of seedlings the following spring. Dead plants can be pulled up and composted.

# OSTEOSPERMUM
## *Osteospermum*

*OSTEOSPERMUM flowers are at their best in full sun in an open situation.*

*CREATE A CARPET OF OSTEOSPERMUM BEDDING in early summer which will continue to flower in flushes until the first frosts. Remember to propagate fresh plants each year.*

## FEATURES

Many varieties of osteospermum can be bought in spring as young plants, but others can be grown from seed and treated as half-hardy annuals. Growing from seed is a cost-effective way of raising large numbers of plants quickly. Favourite plants can be potted-up in autumn and kept in a well-lit frost-free place over winter, then increased by cuttings in spring. In mild areas plants will often survive the winter outdoors and carry on producing a few flowers except in severe spells. In some catalogues it is listed as dimorphotheca. Plants can grow 30–75cm (12–30in) tall.

## CONDITIONS

**Aspect**   Must have full, baking sun for best results.

### OSTEOSPERMUM AT A GLANCE

A hardy/half-hardy annual grown for its brightly-coloured daisy-like flowers that appear all summer. Frost hardy to –5°C (23°F).

| | | RECOMMENDED VARIETIES |
|---|---|---|
| JAN | / | **Osteospermum hybrids:** |
| FEB | / | 'Gaiety' |
| MAR | sow | 'Giant Mixed' |
| APR | sow/transplant | 'Glistening White' |
| MAY | harden off/plant | 'Ink Spot' |
| JUN | flowering | 'Potpourri' |
| JULY | flowering | 'Salmon Queen' |
| AUG | flowering | 'Starshine' |
| SEPT | flowering | 'Tetra Pole Star' |
| OCT | flowering | |
| NOV | / | |
| DEC | / | |

**Site**   Is not fussy about soil but it must be very well-drained. A sheltered spot with the sun beating down all day is ideal. Plants also perform well in containers and these should be sited in full sun facing south if possible. Use multipurpose compost.

## GROWING METHOD

**Sowing**   March/April is the time to sow, sowing seed thinly in 9cm (3½in) diameter pots of soil-based seed compost, and just covering. Germinate at 18°C (64°F) in a bright spot. Seedlings are transplanted to cell trays or individual 9cm (3½in) pots when large enough to handle. Harden off for two weeks and start planting from mid-May onwards.

**Feeding**   Water well to establish and then water only in long spells of hot, dry weather. Extra feeding is unnecessary, but container-grown plants will benefit from occasional liquid feeds given for the benefit of other plants.

**Problems**   Aphids can attack the leaves, flower stalks and buds so choose a spray containing permethrin and wet both sides of the leaves.

## FLOWERING

**Season**   Flowers appear from early summer onwards with a peak later on when temperatures reach their highest.

**Cutting**   Flowers are unsuitable for cutting.

## AFTER FLOWERING

**General**   After the main flowering give plants an overall clipping to tidy them up and maintain compact growth. Lift and pot favourite plants and keep frost-free over winter.

# PAPAVER NUDICAULE

*Iceland poppy*

*ICELAND POPPY has petals with the texture of crepe paper and a velvety sheen. The centre of the flower is a mass of yellow stamens.*

*THEIR TALL STEMS mean the flowers of Papaver nudicaule waft gently in the breeze, and look good like this, massed in bedding.*

## FEATURES

Varieties of *Papaver nudicaule* are available in a wide range of colours and range from 25–75cm (10–30in) tall depending on variety. They can be treated as either half-hardy annuals or hardy biennials sown in summer or autumn. Tall varieties are used for cutting. Plants sown early flower from April onwards.

## CONDITIONS

**Aspect**    Can be grown in cool and warm areas.
**Site**    Poppies need well-drained but moisture-retentive soil with plenty of rotted organic matter added ahead of planting or sowing.

### PAPAVER AT A GLANCE

A hardy biennial (or half-hardy annual) grown for its large showy flowers which appear in summer. Frost hardy to −15°C (5°F).

| | | RECOMMENDED VARIETIES |
|---|---|---|
| JAN | / | *Papaver nudicaule:* |
| FEB | / | **Biennials** |
| MAR | / |   'Large Flowered Special |
| APR | sow |   Mixture' |
| MAY | flowers/sow |   'Meadow Pastels' |
| JUN | flowers/sow |   'Red Sails' |
| JULY | flowering |   'Wonderland Mixed' |
| AUG | flowering | |
| SEPT | flowers/sow | |
| OCT | plant | **Half-hardy annuals** |
| NOV | / |   'Summer Breeze' |
| DEC | / | |

## GROWING METHOD

**Sowing**    Sow seed outdoors April–June or in September. Scatter the seed thinly along shallow drills 1cm (½in) deep, and rake over with fine soil. Thin out when seedlings are 5cm (2in) high, so that the spacing is ultimately at about 15–30cm (6–12in) intervals by October. Do not disturb the fine roots when thinning out, and always water when finished to settle plants back in. Thin autumn-sown poppies in spring in case of winter losses. For earlier flowers sow in pots at 15°C (60°F) in February and grow in cell-trays, planting in late May.

**Feeding**    Extra feeding not needed.

**Problems**    Autumn-sown plants may rot off in heavy soils, so sow in cell trays and keep dry in a coldframe over winter, planting out in spring.

## FLOWERING

**Season**    Flowers appear during early summer and should be picked off as they fade.

**Cutting**    Excellent cut flower. Pick when buds are just opening. Singe stem ends before arranging.

## AFTER FLOWERING

**General**    Leave a few plants to self-seed, but otherwise pull up after the flowers are finished.

# PAPAVER RHOEAS

*Shirley poppy*

*THE UNOPENED BUDS of Shirley poppies gradually rise up from amongst the leaves before bursting open as the petals unfurl.*

*WHEN ALLOWED TO self-seed, poppies will come up amongst other plants. Unwanted plants are very easily pulled out.*

## FEATURES

Shirley poppies, varieties of *Papaver rhoeas*, generally grow to about 60cm (2ft) high, have a very delicate appearance and come in a wide range of colours including pastels. There are single or double varieties and they look effective in large drifts, but can also be sown in patches 30–60cm (1–2ft) across and used as fillers in mixed borders. Each flower can be 7.5cm (3in) across. A hardy annual.

### PAPAVER AT A GLANCE

Shirley poppies are hardy annuals sown in spring or autumn and grown for their large flowers. Frost hardy to –15°C (5°F).

| | | RECOMMENDED VARIETIES |
|---|---|---|
| JAN | / | *Papaver rhoeas:* |
| FEB | / | 'Angels Choir Mixed' |
| MAR | sow | 'Angel Wings Mixed' |
| APR | sow/thin | 'Mother of Pearl' |
| MAY | flowers/sow | 'Selected Single Mixed' |
| JUN | flowering | 'Shirley Double Mixed' |
| JULY | flowering | 'Shirley Single Mixed' |
| AUG | flowering | |
| SEPT | flowers/sow | |
| OCT | / | |
| NOV | / | |
| DEC | / | |

## CONDITIONS

| | |
|---|---|
| **Aspect** | Avoid any shade and grow in full sun. |
| **Site** | Must have very well-drained soil. Rotted compost or manure should be added to the soil a few weeks before sowing. |

## GROWING METHOD

| | |
|---|---|
| **Sowing** | The fine seed can either be scattered on the soil and simply raked in, and the area marked with a circle of sand, or it can be sown in short 1cm (½in) deep drills. March–May and September are the sowing times. Gradually thin out the seedlings until they are 30cm (12in) apart, but avoid transplanting as they dislike disturbance. If sowing in autumn leave thinning until the following spring in case of winter losses. |
| **Feeding** | Extra summer feeding is not required, but water thoroughly should plants start to wilt. |
| **Problems** | Trouble-free. |

## FLOWERING

| | |
|---|---|
| **Season** | Autumn-sown plants flower from late spring onwards, while spring-sown flower in summer. |
| **Cutting** | Suitable as a cut flower if stems are scalded before arranging. |

## AFTER FLOWERING

| | |
|---|---|
| **General** | Leave a few plants to die down and self-seed. |

# PELARGONIUM
*Bedding geranium*

DARK ZONED LEAVES *and an enticing range of single and two-tone flower colours are characteristic of 'Avanti Mixed'.*

YOU MAY BE SURPRISED *to see an ivy-leaved geranium as good as 'Summertime Lilac' coming true from seed.*

## FEATURES

Better known as geraniums, seed-raised pelargoniums are available with large bright flowerheads for bedding, and also as trailing 'ivy-leaved' types. Seeds are sown January/February and need warmth to succeed, so consider buying them as young plants delivered ready-grown in spring. Varieties for bedding and patio containers grow no more than 30cm (1ft), while ivy-leaved types can spread and trail up to 60cm (2ft). Flowers may be single colours or mixtures – the new 'ripple' varieties are eye-catching. Plant 30–60cm (1–2ft) apart. All are half-hardy annuals.

### PELARGONIUM AT A GLANCE

Half-hardy annuals grown for their flowers and also the attractive ivy-like foliage of some varieties. Frost hardy to 0ºC (32ºF).

| | | |
|---|---|---|
| JAN | sow | |
| FEB | sow | |
| MAR | transplant | |
| APR | pot on | |
| MAY | harden off/plant | |
| JUN | flowering | |
| JULY | flowering | |
| AUG | flowering | |
| SEPT | flowering | |
| OCT | / | |
| NOV | / | |
| DEC | / | |

RECOMMENDED VARIETIES

**Pelargonium hybrids:**
**For bedding**
  'Avanti Mixed'
  'Raspberry Ripple'
  'Ripple Mixed'
  'Sensation Mixed'
  'Stardust Mixed'
  'Video Mixed'
**Ivy-leaved varieties**
  'Summertime Lilac'
  'Summer Showers'

## CONDITIONS

**Aspect**    Must be grown in full sun.
**Site**    Well-prepared soil with rotted compost or manure mixed in gives best results. Soil must be well-drained, and when planting up containers use multipurpose compost with slow-release fertiliser mixed in. Bedding geraniums do well in terracotta containers.

## GROWING METHOD

**Sowing**    Sow January/February in a heated propagator in a guaranteed temperature of 18ºC (64ºF). Seedlings appear in 2–3 weeks and can be transplanted to 7.5cm (3in) pots or cell trays of multipurpose compost. Plants must have good light and a temperature of 16–18ºC (61–64ºF) to grow well. Pot on into 10–12.5cm (4–5in) diameter pots, harden off in late May and plant out after the last frosts.
**Feeding**    Liquid feed bedding plants every 2–3 weeks.
**Problems**    Heavy wet soils can lead to rotting of the stems, so grow in containers. Snap off faded flowerheads to avoid grey mould.

## FLOWERING

**Season**    Flowers appear from early summer onwards.
**Cutting**    Not suitable.

## AFTER FLOWERING

**General**    Pull up and compost. Favourite plants can be kept dry and frost-free over winter.

# PETUNIA
## *Petunia*

*'FANTASY MIXED' is the latest in a new range of 'milliflora' petunias with 2.5cm (1in) flowers, ideal for containers and baskets.*

*MULTIFLORA PETUNIAS such as 'Summer Morn Mixed' have 5cm (2in) flowers and are suited to large patio tubs and bedding.*

## FEATURES

Petunias come in a wide range of different types depending on whether they are raised from seed or bought as young plants. Most petunias are perennials grown as half-hardy annuals. Seed-raised varieties fall into the following groups: Millifloras – small flowers 2.5cm (1in) across on compact mounds, for containers and hanging baskets; Multifloras – plenty of 5cm (2in) wide flowers on bushy plants. For bedding and patio containers, with good weather resistance; Floribundas – intermediate in size between multifloras and grandifloras with 7.5cm (3in) flowers; Grandifloras – large trumpet-like 12.5cm (5in) flowers which can bruise in heavy rain and are best for containers in a sheltered position. These all grow 23–30cm (9-12in) tall and can spread up to 60cm (2ft), and are also available as double-flowered varieties. Plant 23–30cm (9–12in) apart. Flower colour varies from single shades to striped, picotee and other variations. Many seed-raised varieties are also widely available as young plants.

An increasing number of petunias are only available as young plants, setting no seed. These are suited to container growing, and include many large double-flowered 'patio' varieties such as 'Able Mabel' and the vigorous Surfinias which can trail to 1.2–1.5m (4–5ft) – see page 78.

### PETUNIA AT A GLANCE

A half-hardy annual grown for all-round use in summer bedding, hanging baskets and containers. Frost hardy to 0°C (5°F).

| | | |
|---|---|---|
| JAN | sow | |
| FEB | sow | |
| MAR | sow/transplant | |
| APR | pot on/grow on | |
| MAY | harden off/plant | |
| JUN | flowering | |
| JULY | flowering | |
| AUG | flowering | |
| SEPT | flowering | |
| OCT | / | |
| NOV | / | |
| DEC | / | |

**RECOMMENDED VARIETIES**

*Petunia hybrida:*
**Millifloras**
  'Fantasy Mixed'
**Multifloras**
  'Celebrity Bunting'
  'Summer Morn Mixed'
**Floribundas**
  'Mirage Mixed'
  'Niagara Mixture'
**Grandifloras**
  'Daddy Mixed'
  'Lavender Storm'

## CONDITIONS

**Aspect** Choose a sunny, south-facing situation for petunias in beds and containers.

**Site** Avoid spots exposed to wind which damages

*PETUNIA 'ABLE MABEL' is the first of a revolutionary new type of double-flowered 'patio' petunia available only as young plants.*

the flowers. Light, free-draining soil with rotted compost/manure mixed in is best. In containers use multipurpose compost.

## GROWING METHOD

**Sowing**  Sowing can take place January–March where a temperature of 21°C (70°F) is possible. Sow onto the level surface of a 9cm (3½in) pot of multipurpose compost, but do not cover seeds, and keep in the light. Seedlings will appear inside two weeks, and should be transplanted to cell trays of multipurpose compost when large enough. Pot on into 9cm (3½in) diameter pots, grow-on and harden off before planting out in early June.

**Feeding**  Give a weekly liquid feed with a high-potash fertiliser to encourage flowers. Mix slow-release fertiliser granules with container compost.

**Problems**  Slugs eat leaves in wet weather – use pellets or slug traps. Plants with mottled, crinkled leaves affected by virus should be destroyed.

## FLOWERING

**Season**  Flowers appear all summer. Pick off dead flowers regularly.

**Cutting**  Not suitable.

## AFTER FLOWERING

**General**  Remove when flowers end.

*FOR A TOUCH OF the patriotic, 'Celebrity Bunting' is a stunning multiflora variety with blend of red, white and blue flowers.*

# PHLOX
*Annual phlox*

*'TWINKLE MIXED' is a striking variety of annual phlox growing around 15cm (6in) tall with star-like flowers in various shades.*

*THE FLOWERS OF annual phlox open at their peak to make rounded heads of colour that can completely fill summer containers.*

## FEATURES

Annual phlox are versatile plants which can be used for bedding, containers and as unique cut flowers. They are half-hardy annuals, growing between 10–45cm (4–18in) tall depending on the variety – taller are better for cutting. Flower colour ranges from the blue of 'Bobby Sox' to the varied shades of 'Tapestry' which is also scented. Several varieties are now available as young plants by mail order. Flowers are long-lived and plants are easy to care for.

### PHLOX AT A GLANCE

A half-hardy annual grown for its heads of colourful flowers, for bedding, containers and for cutting. Frost hardy to –5°C (23°F).

| | | RECOMMENDED VARIETIES |
|---|---|---|
| JAN | / | *Phlox drummondii:* |
| FEB | sow | 'African Sunset' |
| MAR | sow/transplant | 'Bobby Sox' |
| APR | grow on | 'Bright Eyes' |
| MAY | harden off/plant | 'Brilliant' |
| JUN | flowering | 'Cecily Old & New Shades' |
| JULY | flowering | 'Double Chanel' |
| AUG | flowering | 'Phlox of Sheep' |
| SEPT | flowering | 'Tapestry' |
| OCT | / | 'Tutti-Frutti' |
| NOV | / | 'Twinkle Mixed' |
| DEC | / | |

## CONDITIONS

**Aspect**    Needs full sun.
**Site**    Needs well-drained soil with manure or compost mixed in to improve moisture holding. Phlox grow well in multipurpose compost used to fill summer containers.

## GROWING METHOD

**Sowing**    Sow seed in February/March in 9cm (3½in) pots of multipurpose compost, keep at 18°C (64°F), and expect seedlings in 1–3 weeks. Transplant to cell trays or 9cm (3½in) pots, pinch out the tips when 7.5cm (3in) high, and grow on until late May, then harden off and plant after the last frosts in your area.
**Feeding**    Add slow-release fertiliser granules to compost before planting containers, which should be sufficient. Plants in beds can be given a liquid feed every 2–3 weeks in summer.
**Problems**    Plants will struggle on heavy soils in a cold spring so delay planting until warmer weather.

## FLOWERING

**Season**    Flowers appear all summer until frosts.
**Cutting**    Tall varieties are good for cutting and some like 'Tapestry' have a strong, sweet scent.

## AFTER FLOWERING

**General**    Pull up after flowering and compost them.

# PORTULACA
*Sun plant*

*DOUBLE-FLOWERED mixed varieties of portulaca come in a wide range of colours, but attractive single colours are also available.*

*SUN PLANTS can survive the winter in mild seaside gardens, and thrive in the well-drained soil of rockeries.*

## FEATURES

Commonly known as sun plant, portulaca grows 15cm (6in) high with a spreading habit and succulent leaves. The 5cm (2in) flowers open in sun, although modern varieties open even on dull days. It thrives in poor, dry soils and is easily ruined by too much coddling. A half-hardy annual, for beds, pots and rockeries.

## CONDITIONS

**Aspect**     A hot, sunny position gives the best plants.

### PORTULACA AT A GLANCE

Portulaca is a half-hardy annual grown for summer flowers, and gives good results even on thin soils. Frost hardy to 0ºC (32ºF).

| Month | Activity | RECOMMENDED VARIETIES |
|-------|----------|----------------------|
| JAN | / | *Portulaca grandiflora:* |
| FEB | / | 'Cloudbeater Mixed' |
| MAR | sow | 'Double Mixed' |
| APR | sow | 'Kariba Mixed' |
| MAY | harden off/plant | 'Patio Gems' |
| JUN | flowering | 'Sundance' |
| JULY | flowering | 'Sundial Mango' |
| AUG | flowering | 'Sundial Mixed' |
| SEPT | flowering | 'Sundial Peppermint' |
| OCT | / | 'Swanlake' |
| NOV | / | |
| DEC | / | |

**Site**     Unless soil is very well drained plants are prone to rotting. Otherwise plants grow and flower well even where the soil is quite poor – particularly in seaside gardens – as they are adapted to live on little water. Grow them on their own in patio containers, using soil-based potting compost mixed fifty-fifty with sharp grit. Do not feed, and water only when plants start to wilt. Place pots in blazing sunshine.

## GROWING METHOD

**Sowing**     Sow seeds in March/April in 9cm (3½in) pots of soil-based seed compost and germinate at 18ºC (64ºF) in good light. Keep the seedlings on the dry side and transplant to cell trays of soil-based compost with grit added. Grow on, harden off in late May and plant after frosts, watering in well, then only when plants wilt.

**Feeding**     Feeding portulaca is not necessary.

**Problems**     Seedlings will 'damp off' if the compost is kept too wet. If they do fall over, water the pots lightly with a copper-based fungicide.

## FLOWERING

**Season**     Flowers appear throughout summer and into early autumn.

**Cutting**     Not suitable.

## AFTER FLOWERING

**General**     Pull plants up after the first autumn frosts and add their fleshy remains to the compost heap.

# PRIMULA
## *Polyanthus*

*Not an F1 hybrid strain, but 'Giant Superb Mixed' polyanthus are tough, large-flowered and full of character.*

*F1 'Crescendo Mixed' exhibit the clearer, more uniform colours of a highly bred strain, but seed is more expensive.*

## FEATURES

Polyanthus, a hybrid type of primula, is perfect in patio pots or mass planted in the garden for a stunning spring display. Its very brightly coloured flowers up to 5cm (2in) across, on stems 15–30cm (6–12in) tall, rise from neat clumps of bright green, crinkled leaves. A hardy perennial, it is grown as a hardy biennial for spring bedding and containers. Widely available as young plants.

## CONDITIONS

**Aspect**   Grows in full sun or light shade under trees.
**Site**     Needs well-drained soil but with plenty of

organic matter mixed in to help retain moisture – plants do not like to be bone dry at any stage while growing. For containers use multipurpose compost with gravel or chunks of polystyrene put in the base.

## GROWING METHOD

**Sowing**   Polyanthus seed can be tricky to germinate, and the most important rule is not to keep it too warm. Sow in 9cm (3½in) pots of peat-based seed compost from March–July, barely cover, then stand outside in a covered, shaded spot out of the sun. Seedlings will appear 2–3 weeks later. Transplant to cell trays or 9cm (3½in) pots of peat-based potting compost and, pot on into 12.5cm (5in) pots when roots are well developed. Grow during the summer in a shaded spot and do not let them dry out. Plant out in October where flowers are required the following spring, in beds or containers with bulbs and other plants.
**Feeding**  Feed fortnightly with liquid feed in summer.
**Problems** Slugs can devour leaves so use slug pellets. Never bury the crowns or plants may rot.

## FLOWERING

**Season**   Flowers appear earlier in mild winters and carry on throughout spring.
**Cutting**  Charming in spring posies.

## AFTER FLOWERING

**General**  Polyanthus taken from spring displays can be planted in borders where they will form large clumps and flower regularly every spring.

### PRIMULA AT A GLANCE

A hardy biennial grown for its bright spring flowers for use in bedding and containers. Frost hardy to –15°C (5°F).

| | | RECOMMENDED VARIETIES |
|---|---|---|
| JAN | / | **Primula hybrids:** |
| FEB | flowering | 'Crescendo Mixed' |
| MAR | flowers/sow | 'Dobies Superb Mixed' |
| APR | flowers/sow | 'Giant Superb Mixed' |
| MAY | flowers/sow | 'Gold Lace' |
| JUN | sow/grow | 'Harlequin Mixed' |
| JULY | sow/grow | 'Heritage Mixed' |
| AUG | grow | 'Large Flowered Mixed' |
| SEPT | grow | 'Pacific Giants Mixed' |
| OCT | plant | 'Spring Rainbow Mixed' |
| NOV | / | 'Unwins Superb Mixed' |
| DEC | / | |

# RANUNCULUS
*Persian buttercup*

*DOUBLE FLOWERS are characteristic of Ranunculus asiaticus varieties, and are all clear and bright as in this yellow-flowered plant.*

*YOU CAN PLANT ranunculus in beds in spring when the worst of the winter is over, where they will give a bright show of colour.*

## FEATURES

Hardy varieties of *Ranunculus asiaticus* are sown in late summer and autumn for flowers during winter and spring. Seed-raised plants reach around 20–25cm (8–10in) tall. Flowers are double. Young plants are sometimes offered in spring catalogues for delivery in late summer/autumn ready for potting up. Add them to your spring containers as they come into flower – they will grow happily in a cold greenhouse or porch.

### RANUNCULUS AT A GLANCE

A half-hardy annual grown for its large, double, buttercup-like flowers which appear in spring. Frost hardy to –5°C (23°F).

| | | |
|---|---|---|
| JAN | grow | |
| FEB | grow | |
| MAR | flowering | |
| APR | flowering | |
| MAY | flowering | |
| JUN | / | |
| JULY | / | |
| AUG | sow | |
| SEPT | sow/transplant | |
| OCT | sow/grow | |
| NOV | grow | |
| DEC | grow | |

RECOMMENDED VARIETIES

**Ranunculus hybrids:**
'Bloomingdale Mixture'

## CONDITIONS

**Aspect** Give as much sun as possible, and move containers into shelter during stormy or very frosty weather to stop damage to the flowers.

**Site** Use a multipurpose compost for potting up and potting on, and for filling containers if you are creating an 'instant' display as the plants come into flower from early spring.

## GROWING METHOD

**Sowing** Sow seed August–October in 9cm (3½in) pots of peat-based compost, just covering the seeds. Stand outdoors in shade and keep moist – if they get too hot the seeds will not come up. When seedlings appear, bring them into full light and transplant when large enough into 10cm (4in) pots. Grow outdoors until frosts start, then move under protection at night and out during the day. A cool porch is useful. In winter keep plants dry under cover.

**Feeding** Feeding is not usually required.

**Problems** No special problems.

## FLOWERING

**Season** Late winter and throughout spring.

**Cutting** Cut when the buds are just unfurling.

## AFTER FLOWERING

**General** Plants will survive most winters in a sheltered spot and can be planted out in borders.

# RESEDA
## *Mignonette*

*MIGNONETTE FLOWERS individually are insignificant, but the strong sweet fragrance is striking and well worth the effort of sowing.*

*THE FLOWERHEADS of Reseda odorata branch out as they develop. Sow along path edges so the fragrance can be enjoyed.*

## FEATURES

Mignonette has greenish, pink, red, yellow, or coppery flowers and grows to 30cm (12in). It is not particularly striking but is grown mainly for its strong, fruity fragrance – grow it near doors, windows, in patio pots, and near sitting areas to appreciate the qualities of this easily grown hardy annual. It makes a good addition to cottage-style borders.

### RESEDA AT A GLANCE

An easily grown hardy annual grown for its highly fragrant spikes of summer flowers. Frost hardy to –15C (5°F).

| | | |
|---|---|---|
| JAN | / | |
| FEB | / | |
| MAR | sow | |
| APR | sow/thin out | |
| MAY | thin out | |
| JUN | flowering | |
| JULY | flowering | |
| AUG | flowering | |
| SEPT | flowers/sow | |
| OCT | sow | |
| NOV | / | |
| DEC | / | |

**RECOMMENDED VARIETIES**

*Reseda odorata:*
　'Crown Mixture'

　'Machet'
　'Sweet Scented'

## CONDITIONS

**Aspect**　Needs full sun.
**Site**　Needs well-drained soil – dig in organic matter and add lime to acid soils.

## GROWING METHOD

**Sowing**　Seed is sown directly into the ground in short drills 1cm (½in) deep, 15cm (6in) apart. Thin seedlings to 15cm (6in) apart. Sowing can take place in March/April or September/October. Autumn-sown plants need protecting with cloches during cold spells, and should not be thinned until spring. For pots, sow a pinch of seeds in each unit of a cell tray and thin to 2–3 seedlings, grow on and plant up when ready – reseda does not like root disturbance.
**Feeding**　Extra feeding is not usually necessary
**Problems**　Free of troubles.

## FLOWERING

**Season**　Flowers appear from late spring on autumn-sown plants, later on spring-sown.
**Cutting**　Cut when just a few flowers are opening. Dried flowers retain their fragrance.

## AFTER FLOWERING

**General**　Pull plants up when they are past their best, but leave a few to produce seeds and self-sow.

# RICINUS
*Castor oil plant*

*THE VARIETY 'IMPALA' is an excellent choice is you want bold, dark leaves for a dramatic show, growing 1.2m (4ft) tall.*

*BY MIDSUMMER the leaves of ricinus will have formed a dense canopy when grown in beds and planted 60–90cm (2–3ft) apart.*

## FEATURES

A striking and memorable plant grown for its large, lobed, exotic-looking leaves, which are used for bedding, borders and large tubs and containers. The often brightly-coloured summer flowers are followed by spiny seed clusters. By nature an evergreen shrub, ricinus is fast growing and plants are raised fresh from seed each year – in long hot summers they can reach 1.8m (6ft) by 1m (3ft) tall and wide. Annual flowering climbers like thunbergia or ipomoea will climb its stems, their bright orange/blue flowers contrasting with the often deeply coloured ricinus foliage. All parts of the plant are poisonous, especially the seeds. Treat as a half-hardy annual and scrap plants at the end of the summer.

### RICINUS AT A GLANCE

A half-hardy annual with large, exotic leaves in a range of colours, and prized as bold bedder. Frost hardy to 0°C (32°F).

| | | |
|---|---|---|
| JAN | / | |
| FEB | / | |
| MAR | sow | |
| APR | pot on | |
| MAY | harden/plant | |
| JUN | leaves | |
| JULY | leaves | |
| AUG | leaves | |
| SEPT | leaves | |
| OCT | / | |
| NOV | / | |
| DEC | / | |

RECOMMENDED VARIETIES

*Ricinus communis:*
  'Carmencita'
  'Carmencita Pink'
  'Impala'
  'Gibbsonii'
  'Red Spire'
  'Zanzibarensis'

## CONDITIONS

**Aspect**   Must have full sun. In northern areas choose a sheltered, south-facing spot.

**Site**   Soil should be well-drained with plenty of rotted compost or manure dug in. Use loam-based or multipurpose potting compost in containers. In windy spots, stake plants.

## GROWING METHOD

**Sowing**   Soak the hard seeds overnight in warm water, then sow individually in 9cm (3½in) diameter pots of soil-based compost, 5cm (2in) deep in March, and keep at 21°C (70°F). Seedlings appear within three weeks. Pot on into 12.5cm (5in) diameter pots when 15cm (6in) tall. In beds plant 1–1.8m (3–6ft) apart after the last frosts.

**Feeding**   Apply liquid feed weekly from early summer, or mix slow-release fertiliser with the potting compost before planting.

**Problems**   Red spider mite attacks leaves. Wetting the leaves thoroughly every day can help, or use a spray containing bifenthrin.

## FLOWERING

**Season**   The large leaves keep coming all summer long and are joined later by clusters of flowers which rise up above them.

**Cutting**   Leaves are useful for flower arranging, but avoid getting the sap on skin.

## AFTER FLOWERING

**General**   Plants are usually killed by the first frosts of autumn. Ripe seeds can be saved for sowing again the following spring.

# RUDBECKIA
### *Coneflower*

*RUDBECKIA 'RUSTIC DWARFS' is one of the best seed-raised foms. It produces a range of flower colours, yellow through to red, with dark firey centres or cones. Rudbeckia is also known as black-eyed Susan.*

## FEATURES

Rudbeckia or coneflower is one of the easiest and most versatile of all annuals. Try tiny 'Toto' at just 20cm (8in) in patio containers, or, where space allows, 'Indian Summer' at 90cm (3ft). There are intermediate varieties in many shades, and some have an unusual and striking green centre or 'cone'. Half-hardy.

## CONDITIONS

**Aspect**   Rudbeckias need full sun to succeed.
**Site**   Soil must be well-drained but have rotted
compost or manure worked in before planting out. For container growing use multipurpose compost with slow-release fertiliser mixed in.

## RUDBECKIA AT A GLANCE

Grown for its large, showy flowers, rudbeckia grows well in bedding/containers and is half-hardy. Frost hardy to –15°C (5°F).

| | | RECOMMENDED VARIETIES |
|---|---|---|
| JAN | / | *Rudbeckia hirta:* |
| FEB | sow | **Tall varieties** |
| MAR | sow/transplant | 'Goldilocks' |
| APR | grow on | 'Indian Summer' |
| MAY | harden off/plant | 'Marmalade' |
| JUN | flowering | 'Rustic Dwarfs' |
| JULY | flowering | **Short varieties** |
| AUG | flowering | 'Becky Mixed' |
| SEPT | flowering | 'Sonora' |
| OCT | flowering | 'Toto' |
| NOV | / | **Green cone/centre** |
| DEC | / | 'Irish Eyes' |

## GROWING METHOD

**Sowing**   Sow February/March in pots of multipurpose compost and keep at 18°C (64°F). Seedlings appear in 1–2 weeks and are fast growing, soon ready for transplanting into cell trays or 9cm (3½in) pots. Pot larger varieties on into 12.5cm (5in) pots when roots fill the pots, and grow outdoors from mid-May, covering with garden fleece at night if frosty. Plant 15–60cm (6–24in) apart after the last frosts.
**Feeding**   Rudbeckias are strong growers and need little extra feeding in the soil, but give container plants a fortnightly liquid feed unless fertiliser granules are mixed with the compost first.
**Problems**   Slugs can attack after planting so protect with slug pellets or a barrier of sharp grit.

## FLOWERING

**Season**   Summer is the peak period for flowering and regular removal of faded heads should ensure some colour right up to the first autumn frosts.
**Cutting**   Good for cutting because of its strong stems. 'Sonora' is especially good, and 'Indian Summer' has flowers up to 20cm (8in) across.

## AFTER FLOWERING

**General**   Pull plants up and use for compost when they have been knocked down by frosts.

# SALPIGLOSSIS
## *Salpiglossis*

PETAL VEINING *in salpiglossis is intricate and gives rise to the common name of painted tongue. Many different colours are available.*

THE EXOTIC LOOK *can be had by growing mixed salpiglossis in large bold drifts. Choose a variety like 'Casino' at just 45cm (18in).*

## FEATURES

Salpiglossis blooms are trumpet-shaped and come in a range of colours, all with patterned veins. They must have shelter and warmth to do well, so for guaranteed success use them in containers on sunny patios or in south-facing beds protected from the wind. Choose mixed colours or try dark brown 'Chocolate Pot', striking 'Kew Blue' or even the blue/yellow mix 'Chili Blue'. Half-hardy, growing up to 60cm (2ft). Available as young plants.

## CONDITIONS

**Aspect**     Must be in full sun and protected from wind.

### SALPIGLOSSIS AT A GLANCE

Half-hardy annual grown for its exotic flowers but needing a sheltered spot in the garden to do well. Frost hardy to 0°C (32°F).

| | | RECOMMENDED VARIETIES |
|---|---|---|
| JAN | / | *Salpiglossis sinuata:* |
| FEB | sow |   'Batik' |
| MAR | transplant/sow |   'Bolero' |
| APR | grow on |   'Carnival' |
| MAY | harden off/plant |   'Casino' |
| JUN | flowering |   'Chili Blue' |
| JULY | flowering |   'Chocolate Pot'/ |
| AUG | flowering |   'Chocolate Royale' |
| SEPT | flowering |   'Festival Mixed' |
| OCT | / |   'Flamenco Mixed' |
| NOV | / |   'Kew Blue' |
| DEC | / |   'Triumph Mixed' |

**Site**          Drainage must be good or plants will rot – prepare soil by digging in plenty of rotted manure or compost well before planting. Use multipurpose compost in containers and make sure there is a 5cm (2in) layer of gravel in the base to guarantee good drainage. Support plants with twigs or short canes as they get taller and begin to flower.

## GROWING METHOD

**Sowing**     Sow in a 9cm (3½in) pot in February/March and just cover the fine seed. Keep at a temperature of 24°C (75°F) in a light place, and when seedlings are large enough transplant to cell trays or 9cm (3½in) pots. Grow on and then harden off in late May before planting after frosts in early June. Plants are quite brittle so handle carefully.

**Feeding**    Little additional feeding should be needed for plants in bedding displays, but containers can be liquid fed every two weeks if slow-release fertiliser is not used, otherwise just water well.

**Problems**   The flowers are very prone to bruising and damage by wind and heavy rain, so pick off casualties after unsettled spells to avoid an attack by grey mould which can cause rotting.

## FLOWERING

**Season**     Flowers appear throughout the summer.
**Cutting**    Weak stemmed as a cut flower.

## AFTER FLOWERING

**General**    Pull up after autumn frosts and compost.

# SALVIA
## *Scarlet sage*

*IF BRIGHT RED hurts your eyes, try one of the newer mixed salvia varieties containing more subtle shades of mauve, pink and salmon.*

*TO APPRECIATE SALVIAS to the full, grow them in wide, low pans on the patio and keep fed and watered throughout the summer.*

## FEATURES

*Salvia splendens* or scarlet sage is used in bold groups in bedding and is also a useful container plant. Most varieties grow to 30cm (1ft) with similar spread, but giants like 'Rambo' with red flowers reach 60cm (2ft). Flowers are long and tubular, in spikes, and colours other than the typical vibrant red include pink, mauve, salmon, pastel shades and even bicolours such as 'Salsa Bicolour Mixed' with white tipped blooms. Choose single colours or mixtures. Grown as a half-hardy annual but is in fact a perennial plant. Several varieties are usually available as young plants by mail order.

### SALVIA AT A GLANCE

A half-hardy annual grown for its often bright and brash flowers which are useful for bedding and pots. Frost hardy to 0°C (32°F).

| | | RECOMMENDED VARIETIES |
|---|---|---|
| JAN | / | *Salvia splendens:* |
| FEB | sow | 'Blaze of Fire' |
| MAR | sow/transplant | 'Firecracker' |
| APR | grow on | 'Orange Zest' |
| MAY | harden off/plant | 'Phoenix Mixed' |
| JUN | flowering | 'Phoenix Purple' |
| JULY | flowering | 'Rambo' |
| AUG | flowering | 'Red Arrow' |
| SEPT | flowering | 'Scarlet King' |
| OCT | / | 'Scarlet O'Hara' |
| NOV | / | 'Sizzler Burgundy' |
| DEC | / | 'Sizzler Mixed' |

## CONDITIONS

**Aspect** Plant salvias in a warm spot in full sun.
**Site** Tolerates a wide range of soils but drainage must be very good or plants may rot. Mix in well-rotted compost or manure before planting and use multipurpose compost for filling patio pots and windowboxes. Make sure plastic containers have drainage holes, and drill some if necessary, then put in 5cm (2in) of gravel.

## GROWING METHOD

**Sowing** February/March is the time to sow salvias, using 9cm (3½in) pots of multipurpose compost. Lightly cover seeds and keep in a bright spot such as a windowsill at 18°C (64°F); expect seedlings in 2–3 weeks. Transplant into cell trays or 10cm (4in) pots, grow on, harden off in late May before planting 15–30cm (6–12in) apart.
**Feeding** Liquid feed plants in beds monthly. Mix slow-release fertiliser with compost at planting.
**Problems** Heavy wet soils can cause root rots, and slugs and snails will eat leaves of young plants in damp and wet spells. Use slug pellets.

## FLOWERING

**Season** Cut faded spikes right back and plants will often produce a succession of flowers right into the late summer months.
**Cutting** Not suitable.

## AFTER FLOWERING

**General** Dig out when over and compost.

# SCABIOSA

*Sweet scabious*

*FOR A COTTAGE GARDEN feel make sure you include pink scabious heads with other plants such as this white candytuft.*

*AS A BORDER FILLER sweet scabious is very useful and can be sown in any gaps during March and April for flowers from June.*

## FEATURES

Also known as pincushion flower, varieties of *Scabiosa atropurpurea* are easily grown hardy annuals. The rounded flowerheads come in shades of blue, mauve, purple, pink, white or crimson. Growing to 30–50cm (12–20in) with tall, wire-like stems, scabious is best used for growing in big patches and for use as a filler in between other plants in a mixed or cottage-garden style border. A related variety, 'Paper Moon', is grown for its spherical heads of dry bracts which follow the flowers.

### SCABIOSA AT A GLANCE

An easily-grown hardy annual with rounded flowerheads that are useful in borders and for cutting. Frost hardy to -15°C (5°F).

| | | |
|---|---|---|
| JAN | / | **RECOMMENDED VARIETIES** |
| FEB | / | |
| MAR | sow | *Scabiosa atropurpurea:* |
| APR | sow/thin out | 'Ace of Spades' |
| MAY | thin out | 'Border Hybrids' |
| JUN | flowers/thin out | 'Dobies Giant Hybrids' |
| JULY | flowering | 'Double Mixed' |
| AUG | flowering | 'Dwarf Double Mixed' |
| SEPT | flowering | 'Tall Double' |
| OCT | / | |
| NOV | / | *Scabiosa stellata:* |
| DEC | / | 'Paper Moon'/'Ping Pong'/'Drum Stick' |

## CONDITIONS

**Aspect** Prefers full sun and protection from wind.
**Site** Well-drained soil is best – prepare ground by digging in organic matter well in advance.

## GROWING METHOD

**Sowing** Sow outdoors March/April where plants are to flower, in short drills 1cm (½in) deep. Thin plants to 15–30cm (6–12in) apart by early summer, and keep weed free.
**Feeding** Extra feeding in summer is not needed.
**Problems** No particular problems.

## FLOWERING

**Season** Flowers appear from mid- to late summer.
**Cutting** Excellent and long-lasting cut flower.

## AFTER FLOWERING

**General** Pull plants up when they are over.

# SCHIZANTHUS
*Poor man's orchid*

*THE EXOTIC APPEAL of schizanthus earns it the common name of poor man's orchid. Each flower has a network of darker veining.*

*THE FINELY DIVIDED leaves are the perfect foil for the large heads of flowers. Varieties like 'Pierrot' are distinctly dome-shaped.*

## FEATURES

Also known as butterfly flower, schizanthus is stunning when used in bedding or in large pots and troughs. It has fern-like foliage and brilliantly coloured, trumpet-shaped flowers in rich tones of pink, purple, magenta, pastels or white. The flower throats are intricately patterned. Only the dwarf varieties reaching 20–30cm (8–12in) are worth growing outdoors, and they must have shelter from strong winds and the hot midday sun. Schizanthus is a half-hardy annual and very sensitive to even slight frost.

### SCHIZANTHUS AT A GLANCE

A half-hardy annual grown in containers on patios or in south-facing borders for summer flowers. Frost hardy to 0°C (32°F).

| | | |
|---|---|---|
| JAN | / | |
| FEB | / | |
| MAR | sow | |
| APR | transplant | |
| MAY | harden off | |
| JUN | plant/flowers | |
| JULY | flowering | |
| AUG | flowering | |
| SEPT | flowering | |
| OCT | / | |
| NOV | / | |
| DEC | / | |

RECOMMENDED VARIETIES

*Schizanthus pinnatus:*
'Angel Wings Mixed'
'Disco'
'My Lovely'
'Pierrot'
'Star Parade'

## CONDITIONS

**Aspect** — Must be sheltered and have full sun.

**Site** — Well-drained soil that has been enriched before planting with rotted manure or compost produces strong plants. Peat- or coir-based potting compost guarantees good results when containers are used.

## GROWING METHOD

**Sowing** — Seeds are sown in March at 16°C (61°F) in small pots of peat- or coir-based seed compost, and seedlings appear after 1–2 weeks. Transplant to cell trays or 9cm (3½in) pots, grow through spring and plant after hardening off, in early June. Space plants 15–30cm (6–12in) apart. Pinch out growing tips when 10cm (4in) high to make bushy plants.

**Feeding** — Liquid feed monthly, and water containers regularly – if slow-release fertiliser was added to the compost extra feeding is not necessary.

**Problems** — No special problems.

## FLOWERING

**Season** — Flowers reach a peak in mid- to late summer and keep coming if faded stems are removed.

**Cutting** — Not usually used as a cut flower.

## AFTER FLOWERING

**General** — The soft leafy plants soon break down when put on the compost heap.

# SENECIO
*Dusty miller*

*A WHITE WOOLLY LAYER covering the otherwise green leaves gives Senecio cineraria its attractive silvery-grey appearance.*

*OVERWINTERED PLANTS will keep on growing the following season, get larger and also produce heads of bright yellow flowers.*

## FEATURES

Grown for its attractive silver-grey foliage, *Senecio cineraria* is often found listed under 'cineraria' in seed catalogues. Use in bedding schemes and as a foliage container plant. Plants grow up to 30cm (12in) tall and wide in summer, but if left outdoors over winter can be twice that if the yellow flowerheads are allowed to develop. Usually grown as a half-hardy annual, senecio is naturally an evergreen, eventually developing a tough woody base.

### SENECIO AT A GLANCE

Prized for its silver-grey leaves and grown as a foliage bedding plant and for using in containers. Frost hardy to –5°C (23°F).

| | | |
|---|---|---|
| JAN | / | |
| FEB | sow | **RECOMMENDED VARIETIES** |
| MAR | sow | *Senecio cineraria:* |
| APR | transplant | **Fine, divided leaves** |
| MAY | harden off/plant | 'Dwarf Silver' |
| JUN | leaves | 'Silver Dust' |
| JULY | leaves | |
| AUG | leaves | **Rounded leaves** |
| SEPT | leaves | 'Cirrus' |
| OCT | leaves | |
| NOV | / | |
| DEC | / | |

## CONDITIONS

**Aspect** Must have full sun.
**Site** Well-drained soil is needed, but plants do well in light, sandy soils, especially in seaside gardens. Use multipurpose compost in pots.

## GROWING METHOD

**Sowing** Start plants in February/March at 20°C (68°F), by sowing seed in a small pot of compost and just covering. Expect seedlings after 1–2 weeks and keep in good light. Keep compost slightly on the dry side to avoid 'damping off'. Transplant to cell trays or 9cm (3½in) pots, grow on, then harden off at the end of April and plant in May, 30cm (12in) apart.
**Feeding** Planted containers need liquid feed every two weeks, and regular watering. Plants stand dry spells outside but water them if they wilt.
**Problems** If seedlings collapse, give a light watering with a copper-based fungicide.

## FLOWERING

**Season** The silvery leaves are attractive all summer.
**Cutting** Foliage can be used in arrangements.

## AFTER FLOWERING

**General** Pull up and compost in autumn. In many areas plants will survive the winter if left and produce bigger clumps of leaves and flowers.

# SOLENOSTEMON

*Coleus or flame nettle*

*'BLACK DRAGON' is a modern variety of coleus with black-edged, pinkish-red leaves, and is useful for specific colour themes.*

*LEAF COLOUR is apparent from an early age with solenostemon, making it possible to group the different colours when planting.*

## FEATURES

Look under 'coleus' in seed catalogues for a wide range of varieties of this striking foliage plant. A half-hardy annual, solenostemon is a valuable bedding and container plant with large multicoloured leaves that add a certain 'tropical' and eccentric element to summer gardens. As well as mixtures, dark-leaved varieties like 'Black Dragon' can be put to use in colour-themed displays. Size range is 20–45cm (8–18in) depending on variety, and it is important to remove all flowerheads as they appear or the plant will stop producing leaves. Varieties are available as young plants.

## CONDITIONS

**Aspect** Flame nettles need full sun to really thrive and also need shelter from persistent winds.

**Site** Well-drained soil that has had plenty of rotted manure or compost mixed in before planting produces strong plants with good colour. Where they are grown in patio containers use multipurpose compost with slow-release fertiliser granules added at planting time.

## GROWING METHOD

**Sowing** March is the time to sow seed, in 9cm (3½in) pots of multipurpose compost, just scattering the seed on the surface – don't cover. Keep at 24°C (75°F) where they get bright light. Seedlings grow slowly but when they are large enough, transplant to 9cm (3½in) pots or large cell trays. Pinch out the growing tip when plants are 7.5cm (3in) tall to encourage bushy growth and the maximum number of leaves. Harden off in late May and plant after frosts, 15–30cm (6–12in) apart.

**Feeding** Liquid feeding every two weeks during summer maintains vigorous leaf growth. If slow-release fertiliser has been used, feed only monthly with half-strength liquid feed.

**Problems** Slugs and snails attack young plants, so protect with slug pellets or a barrier of sharp grit around each plant.

## FLOWERING

**Season** All flowers should be removed as soon as they appear to encourage maximum leaf growth. Plants generally stay colourful until frosts.

**Cutting** Not suitable.

## AFTER FLOWERING

**General** Favourite plants can be lifted and potted up in autumn, and kept dry over winter in a frost-free greenhouse or cool room. Take cuttings from these plants in spring.

### SOLENOSTEMON AT A GLANCE

A half-hardy annual grown for its brightly-coloured leaves which are used in bedding and for patio pots. Frost hardy to 0°C (32°F).

| Month | Activity | | RECOMMENDED VARIETIES |
|---|---|---|---|
| JAN | / | | *Solenostemon scutellarioides:* |
| FEB | / | | |
| MAR | sow | 🌱 | 'Black Dragon' |
| APR | transplant | 🌱 | 'Camelot Mixed' |
| MAY | harden off/plant | 🌱 | 'Dragon Sunset & Volcano, Mixed' |
| JUN | leaves | 🍃 | 'Fairway' |
| JULY | leaves | 🍃 | 'Flame Dancers' |
| AUG | leaves | 🍃 | 'Magic Lace' |
| SEPT | leaves | 🍃 | 'Salmon Lace' |
| OCT | / | | 'Top Crown' |
| NOV | / | | 'Wizard Mixed' |
| DEC | / | | |

# TAGETES
*Marigold*

*THESE SINGLE-FLOWERED French marigolds are much daintier than their loud cousins with larger double flowers.*

*SINGLE FLOWER COLOURS are useful in colour-themed displays and this double-flowered French marigold would go well with blues.*

## FEATURES

The marigold 'family' is made up of African and French types, and tagetes. All are easily grown half-hardy annuals and their flowers are among some of the loudest available – bright oranges, reds, yellows and bronzes that set borders and containers alight. Plant size varies from 15cm (6in) dwarfs to 90cm (3ft) giants, and there are unusual flower colours such as 'Vanilla' and even bright stripey-petalled varieties such as 'Mr Majestic'. Use them for bold bedding or as reliable patio container plants. Flowers can be single, semi or fully double and up to 7.5cm (3in) across. Many varieties are also available as young plants.

### TAGETES AT A GLANCE

A half-hardy annual grown for its bright flowers which are ideal for bedding and patio pots/troughs. Frost hardy to 0°C (32°F).

| | | |
|---|---|---|
| JAN | / | |
| FEB | sow | |
| MAR | sow | |
| APR | sow/transplant | |
| MAY | harden off/plant | |
| JUN | flowering | |
| JULY | flowering | |
| AUG | flowering | |
| SEPT | flowering | |
| OCT | / | |
| NOV | / | |
| DEC | / | |

RECOMMENDED VARIETIES

**African marigolds**
'Inca Mixed'
'Shaggy Maggy'
'Vanilla'
**French marigolds**
'Boy O'Boy Mixed'
'Mischief Mixed'
'Mr Majestic'
*Tagetes tenuifolia:*
'Lemon Gem'
'Red Gem'

## CONDITIONS

**Aspect**    Must have a sunny position.
**Site**    Marigolds are not too fussy about soils, but mixing in rotted compost before planting helps keep soil moist. For container growing use multipurpose compost with slow-release fertiliser granules mixed well in. Tall varieties of African marigold need shelter from wind.

## GROWING METHOD

**Sowing**    All marigolds can be sown February–April, but a May sowing on a windowsill will also be successful as they are fast growers and soon catch up. Just cover the large seeds with compost and keep at 21°C (70°F). Seedlings will appear in a week and can be transplanted to cell trays. Grow on, harden off in late May and plant after frosts. Nip off any flower buds that appear before and two weeks after planting.
**Feeding**    Fortnightly liquid feeding keeps plants in beds going strong. Keep containers well watered.
**Problems**    Slugs and snails can strip plants overnight so protect with slug pellets in wet/warm spells.

## FLOWERING

**Season**    Early sowings produce earlier flowers and vice-versa. Late sowings provide handy colour in late summer and if grown in pots, plants can be used to revive flagging summer containers.
**Cutting**    African marigolds are useful for cutting.

## AFTER FLOWERING

**General**    Pull plants up when finished and compost.

# THUNBERGIA
## *Black-eyed Susan*

*BLACK-EYED SUSAN is one of the brightest and showiest of all the annual climbers, and readily entwines the stems of other plants. It hates having its roots disturbed so sow seeds straight into small pots, and pot 2–3 plants on together when necessary. Plant out after frosts.*

## FEATURES

The flowers of thunbergia can be orange, yellow or white, and sometimes the black eye is missing altogether. Grow as a half-hardy annual for indoors and out. Outdoors, grow up wigwams of 1.5m (5ft) canes, either in borders, or large tubs for a moveable display of colour. In hanging baskets thunbergia soon entwines the chains, making an effective camouflage. In patio tubs train plants up through other tall annuals like ricinus and sunflowers, or plant them around the base of outdoor plants in early summer. In colder areas grow plants in the conservatory or porch to guarantee a good show of flowers. Seed pods tend to set very easily which reduces the ability of the plant to keep flowering, so nip these off regularly.

### THUNBERGIA AT A GLANCE

A half-hardy annual climber flowering in summer for patio containers, baskets and bedding. Frost hardy to 0°C (32°F).

| | | |
|---|---|---|
| JAN | / | |
| FEB | / | |
| MAR | sow | |
| APR | pot on/grow on | |
| MAY | harden/plant out | |
| JUN | flowers | |
| JULY | flowers | |
| AUG | flowers | |
| SEPT | flowers | |
| OCT | / | |
| NOV | / | |
| DEC | / | |

RECOMMENDED VARIETIES

*Thunbergia alata:*
'Susie Mixed'

## CONDITIONS

**Aspect**  A south-facing spot in full sun is essential. In conservatories direct hot sun should be avoided or the leaves may be scorched.

**Site**  In containers use multipurpose compost with slow-release fertiliser added. Well-drained, moisture retentive soil, with rotted manure or compost is needed outdoors.

## GROWING METHOD

**Sowing**  Soak seeds overnight then sow three to a 9cm (3½in) diameter pot in March. Germinate at 18°C (64°F). Germination is erratic and seedlings may take a month to emerge. A small wigwam of canes will support the shoots. Grow several plants on in large pots during May, then harden off and plant after the last frosts. They dislike root disturbance.

**Feeding**  Liquid feed once a week in summer.

**Problems**  Red spider mite attacks leaves. Wet the leaves daily or use a spray containing pirimiphos-methyl. Indoors use the predator phytoseiulus. Whitefly will feed on the leaves and cause sticky 'honeydew'. Use a spray containing permethrin or the natural encarsia indoors.

## FLOWERING

**Season**  Flowers appear all summer and the flowering period is extended when plants are grown under some form of protection.

**Cutting**  Not suitable.

## AFTER FLOWERING

**General**  Nip off faded flowers. Remove outdoor plants after frosts and add to the compost heap.

# TITHONIA

*Mexican sunflower*

*THE DAHLIA-LIKE FLOWERS of tithonia have an 'exotic' feel to them and each one can be up to 7.5cm (3in) across, on strong stems.*

*THE HEART-SHAPED LEAVES of Mexican sunflower are an added bonus, and each flower also has a distinct swollen 'neck'.*

## FEATURES

Tithonia, as its common name suggests, comes from warmer areas, so does well here when there is plenty of sun. Grow as a half-hardy annual. 'Fiesta del Sol' is just 30cm (1ft) tall, while 'Torch' can reach 1.2m (4ft). Flowers are large, exotic-looking and dahlia-like, red-orange, and have a distinct swollen 'neck'.

## CONDITIONS

**Aspect**   Must have full sun or plants will suffer.

### TITHONIA AT A GLANCE

A half-hardy annual grown for its large orange flowers held on strong stems. Use in bedding and pots. Frost hardy to 0°C (32°F).

| | | RECOMMENDED VARIETIES |
|---|---|---|
| JAN | / | |
| FEB | sow | *Tithonia rotundifolia:* |
| MAR | sow | **Tall varieties** |
| APR | sow/transplant |   'Goldfinger' |
| MAY | harden off/plant |   'Torch' |
| JUN | flowering | |
| JULY | flowering | **Short varieties** |
| AUG | flowering |   'Fiesta del Sol' |
| SEPT | flowering | |
| OCT | / | |
| NOV | / | |
| DEC | / | |

**Site**   Not fussy about soil, but needs good drainage. Plant in a fairly sheltered spot away from cold driving winds. Tithonia has a tendency to go pale and yellow when growing conditions are poor. Grow plants in containers if the soil is heavy, using multipurpose compost.

## GROWING METHOD

**Sowing**   Sow seeds February to April in 9cm (3½in) pots of multipurpose compost, just covering them, and germinate at 18°C (64°F) in a warm place or heated propagator. Transplant to individual 9cm (3½in) pots or large cell trays and grow on. Harden off for 2–3 weeks and plant in early summer when the soil warms up. If seedlings or young plants turn yellow they are being kept too cold. Can also be sown outdoors in early June where plants are to flower.

**Feeding**   Feed container-grown plants twice a month with liquid feed.

**Problems**   Slugs may attack the leaves after early summer rains so protect with slug pellets.

## FLOWERING

**Season**   Flowers appear from midsummer and later sowings continue to give colour into autumn.

**Cutting**   Suitable for use as a cut flower.

## AFTER FLOWERING

**General**   Pull up after flowering. May self-seed.

# TORENIA
*Wishbone flower*

*WISHBONE FLOWER gets its common name from the dark markings found on the lower lip of the flowers of some varieties.*

*SHELTER IS ESSENTIAL for success with torenia, which can also be potted up and grown-on as a flowering plant for indoors.*

## FEATURES

Wishbone flower needs to be in the 'front row' of a summer bedding scheme, or used around the edge of pots and troughs. The variety 'Susie Wong' has bright yellow flowers with black throats, and a spreading habit making it ideal for baskets. Half-hardy annuals, torenias grow no more than 30cm (1ft) in height.

## CONDITIONS

**Aspect**    Choose a sheltered spot with sun.

### TORENIA AT A GLANCE

A low growing half-hardy annual grown for its colourful lipped flowers, for edging in beds and pots. Frost hardy to 0°C (32°F).

|  |  |
|-------|----------|
| JAN | / |
| FEB | / |
| MAR | sow |
| APR | sow/transplant |
| MAY | grow/harden off |
| JUN | plant/flowers |
| JULY | flowering |
| AUG | flowering |
| SEPT | flowering |
| OCT | / |
| NOV | / |
| DEC | / |

RECOMMENDED VARIETIES

*Torenia fournieri:*
 'Clown Mixed'
 'Susie Wong'

**Site**    Dig in rotted manure or compost a few weeks ahead of planting out, or use multipurpose compost for container growing. Soil and compost used must be free draining. Avoid planting where winds are persistent.

## GROWING METHOD

**Sowing**    Sow the very small seeds in pots or trays in March/April, barely cover and keep at 18°C (64°F) in a well-lit place. When large enough the seedlings can be transplanted to cell trays and grown on until late May, then hardened off and planted well after the last frosts, 15cm (6in) apart, or in groups in patio pots. Plant five plants to a 40cm (16in) diameter hanging basket, four around the sides and one in the centre. 'Susie Wong' will creep in and out of other plants.

**Feeding**    Feed regularly every 2–3 weeks with a balanced liquid plant food.

**Problems**    Trouble free.

## FLOWERING

**Season**    Throughout summer.

**Cutting**    Not used as a cut flower.

## AFTER FLOWERING

**General**    Pull or dig out the plants once flowering has stopped. They will sometimes self-seed, and they will then produce seedlings in the following year.

# TROPAEOLUM
## *Nasturtium*

*'MOONLIGHT' is a climbing variety of nasturtium reaching 1.8m (6ft) with soft yellow flowers against light green leaves.*

*FOR DOUBLE VALUE grow 'Alaska Mixed' with light green leaves speckled with creamy-white, plus red and yellow flowers.*

## FEATURES

With big seeds and quick growth, tropaeolum, better known as nasturtium, is one of the easiest of all hardy annuals to grow. Plants just 23cm (9in) tall are perfect for bedding and patio planters, while others will scramble up thought a dull hedge. The colour range is huge, and single and mixed colours are available. For pretty leaves too, grow 'Alaska Mixed' which is speckled with white.

### TROPAEOLUM AT A GLANCE

A hardy annual grown for its colourful flowers and often variegated leaves. For beds and containers. Frost hardy to 0°C (32°F).

| | | RECOMMENDED VARIETIES |
|---|---|---|
| JAN | / | *Tropaeolum majus:* |
| FEB | sow | **Tall climbers** |
| MAR | sow | 'Climbing Mixed' |
| APR | transplant | 'Jewel of Africa' |
| MAY | transplant | **Short, mixed colours** |
| JUN | flowering | 'Alaska Mixed' |
| JULY | flowering | 'Gleam Mixed' |
| AUG | flowering | 'Tip Top Mixed' |
| SEPT | flowering | **Single colours** |
| OCT | / | 'Empress of India' |
| NOV | / | 'Gleaming Mahogany' |
| DEC | / | 'Moonlight' |

## CONDITIONS

**Aspect**  Needs full sun.
**Site**  Poor, thin soil gives excellent results when grown under hedges or in bedding displays.

## GROWING METHOD

**Sowing**  Simply push the large seeds 2.5–5cm (1–2in) into the soil in April, in groups of 3–5 where plants are to flower. Fleshy seedlings appear 2–3 weeks later and they can all be left to develop and form a large clump. If needed for containers, sow three seeds to a 9cm (3½in) pot at the same time and keep warm until seedlings appear, then keep outdoors.
**Feeding**  Feeding encourages leaves at the expense of flowers, although if other plants are growing in a container or basket, some extra feeding is unavoidable. Don't feed plants growing in soil.
**Problems**  Aphids and caterpillars feed under the leaves, so check regularly and squash if seen.

## FLOWERING

**Season**  Flowering is all summer long.
**Cutting**  Not used cut, but flowers and the peppery leaves can be used raw in summer salads.

## AFTER FLOWERING

**General**  Pull up and compost. Self-seeds very easily.

# VERBENA
## *Verbena*

*SOFTER PASTEL SHADES can be found in modern varieties of verbena – these are just a few flowers of the variety 'Romance Pastels'.*

*'PEACHES & CREAM' has a unique colour that makes it a real winner, at 20cm (8in), for patio containers and hanging baskets.*

## FEATURES

Most verbenas grow 15–30cm (6–12in) tall and are prized for their heads of bright flowers. Mixtures or single shades like 'Peaches & Cream' are used for planting containers or for bedding. Raise from seed – although this is tricky – or grow them from mail order plants. Most trailing verbenas are not seed raised but bought as ready-grown plants from garden centres and mail order catalogues in spring.

### VERBENA AT A GLANCE

A half-hardy annual used in bedding and containers. Masses of bright flowers appear during summer. Frost hardy to 0°C (32°F).

| | | |
|---|---|---|
| JAN | / | |
| FEB | / | |
| MAR | sow | |
| APR | transplant | |
| MAY | grow/harden off | |
| JUN | flowering | |
| JULY | flowering | |
| AUG | flowering | |
| SEPT | flowering | |
| OCT | / | |
| NOV | / | |
| DEC | / | |

**RECOMMENDED VARIETIES**

*Verbena hybrida:*
**Mixed colours**
'Crown Jewels'
'Novalis Mixed'
'Raspberry Crush'
'Romance Pastels'
**Single colours**
'Adonis Blue'
'Apple Blossom'
'Peaches & Cream'
**Spreading/trailing**
'Misty'

## CONDITIONS

**Aspect** Needs full sun for best results.
**Site** Use multipurpose compost in containers, and mix rotted compost with soil outdoors.

## GROWING METHOD

**Sowing** To succeed with verbena seed, sow on the surface of peat-based seed compost in March and cover the seeds with a thin layer of fine vermiculite. Water and keep at 21°C (70°F). Seedlings appear 2–3 weeks later, and should be kept slightly on the dry side. When large enough, transplant seedlings to cell trays or individual 7.5cm (3in) pots, and grow on. Plant after hardening off in late spring/early summer.
**Feeding** Feed monthly with balanced liquid feed.
**Problems** Powdery mildew can attack leaves – use a spray containing sulphur at the first signs.

## FLOWERING

**Season** Flowers appear all summer.
**Cutting** Not used for cutting.

## AFTER FLOWERING

**General** Pull up when finished and use for compost.

# VIOLA CORNUTA

## Viola

DIMINUTIVE 'Bambini' violas are guaranteed to steal your heart with their inquisitive whiskery faces.

FOR A TOUCH OF DRAMA try combining the moody 'Blackjack' with a clear yellow variety in a hanging basket.

## FEATURES

Violas are smaller than pansies but they are no less prolific, and what they lack in size they make up for in sheer character. Most are varieties of *Viola cornuta*, and all are quite hardy, being sown in spring or summer. Grow single colours, mixtures like 'Bambini', or trailing yellow 'Sunbeam' for hanging baskets. Violas grow to around 15cm (6in), making bushy little plants for bedding or containers. Try planting them in cottage style wicker baskets. Available as young plants.

### VIOLA AT A GLANCE

A hardy annual grown for its pretty little pansy flowers which appear on branching plants. Frost hardy to –15°C (5°F).

| | | RECOMMENDED VARIETIES |
|---|---|---|
| JAN | / | **Viola hybrids:** |
| FEB | sow | 'Bambini Mixed' |
| MAR | sow | 'Blackjack' |
| APR | sow/flower | 'Blue Moon' |
| MAY | sow/flower | 'Cuty' |
| JUN | sow/flower | 'Juliette Mixed' |
| JULY | sow/flower | 'Midnight Runner' |
| AUG | grow on/flowers | 'Princess Mixed' |
| SEPT | grow on/flowers | 'Sorbet Yesterday, Today |
| OCT | plant | & Tomorrow' |
| NOV | / | 'Sunbeam' |
| DEC | / | |

## CONDITIONS

**Aspect**
**Site**
Grows well in sun or dappled, light shade. Soil does not need to be over prepared, but must be well-drained. For container growing use multipurpose compost.

## GROWING METHOD

**Sowing**
Sow from February under cover for flowers the same summer, or outside May–July for flowers the following spring. Either way, sow in a 9cm (3½in) pot of multipurpose compost and barely cover seeds. In early spring keep at 15°C (60°F) and transplant seedlings when large enough to cell trays, grow, harden off and plant in late May. When summer sowing, stand the pot outside in shade to germinate then treat seedlings the same, planting out in October where you want the plants to flower.

**Feeding**
Extra feeding is not usually necessary.

**Problems**
Use slug pellets if the leaves are attacked.

## FLOWERING

**Season**
Spring-sown plants flower during summer, summer-sown the following spring/summer.

**Cutting**
The delicate cut stems of 'Queen Charlotte' are sometimes used for making scented posies.

## AFTER FLOWERING

**General**
Plants often carry on as short-lived perennials, and also self-seed freely.

# VIOLA TRICOLOR
## *Wild pansy*

*EACH FLOWER of wild pansy is like a tiny whiskered 'face' and individual plants all vary from each other very slightly.*

*ONE PLANT left in the ground to mature through the summer will shed hundreds of seeds which will germinate the next spring.*

## FEATURES

*Viola tricolor* is the wild pansy, also known commonly as heartsease or Johnny-jump-up. It is usually grown as a hardy annual but can also be treated as a biennial. Much daintier than its relatives the pansies, these plants are at home in cottage-style beds and as pot edging. A few single coloured varieties are available, such as the unusual 'Bowles' Black', having black flowers with a small central yellow 'eye'.

### VIOLA AT A GLANCE

A hardy annual grown for its pretty little pansy flowers which appear on branching plants. Frost hardy to –15°C (5°F).

| | | RECOMMENDED VARIETIES |
|---|---|---|
| JAN | / | |
| FEB | sow | *Viola tricolor* |
| MAR | sow | **Single colours:** |
| APR | sow/flower | Blue |
| MAY | sow/flower | 'Prince Henry' |
| JUN | sow/flower | Yellow |
| JULY | sow/flower | 'Prince John' |
| AUG | grow on/flowers | |
| SEPT | grow on/flowers | |
| OCT | plant | |
| NOV | / | |
| DEC | / | |

## CONDITIONS

**Aspect** — Grows well sun or dappled, light shade.
**Site** — Soil does not need to be over prepared, but must be well-drained. Multipurpose compost is best for growing *Viola tricolor* in containers.

## GROWING METHOD

**Sowing** — Sow from February under cover for flowers the same summer, or outside May–July for flowers the following spring. Either way, sow in a 9cm (3½in) pot of multipurpose compost and barely cover seeds. In early spring keep at 15°C (60°F) and transplant seedlings when large enough to cell trays, grow, harden off and plant in late May. When summer sowing, stand the pot outside in shade to germinate, treat seedlings the same, and plant in October.

**Feeding** — Extra feeding is not usually necessary.
**Problems** — Use slug pellets if the leaves are attacked.

## FLOWERING

**Season** — Spring-sown plants flower during summer, summer-sown the following spring/summer.
**Cutting** — Not suitable for cutting.

## AFTER FLOWERING

**General** — Pull plants up and compost, or leave a few to shed seeds. They will sometimes grow as perennials and last for several years.

# VIOLA WITTROCKIANA
## *Pansy*

*PANSY FLOWERS have 'faces' that tend to face the sun, especially in early spring. Use them in patio pots with bulbs like tulips.*

*'JOLLY JOKER' is a unique and prolific variety of summer-flowering pansy with orange and rich royal purple two-tone flowers.*

## FEATURES

Pansies are hardy and will flower almost all year round. There are two groups, summer flowering, and autumn/winter flowering. None grow more than 20cm (8in) tall. Flowers are like large flat 'faces' up to 7.5cm (3in) across. Colours vary enormously from single, pastel shades to striking bicolours, and are available in mixtures or as single colours. Many varieties are available as young plants by mail order. Most are varieties of *Viola wittrockiana*.

### VIOLA AT A GLANCE

Hardy and grown either as an annual or a biennial for flowers in summer and autumn/winter. Frost hardy to −15°C (5°F).

| | | |
|---|---|---|
| JAN | / | |
| FEB | sow | |
| MAR | sow | |
| APR | sow/flower | |
| MAY | sow/flower | |
| JUN | sow/flower | |
| JULY | sow/flower | |
| AUG | grow on/flowers | |
| SEPT | grow on/flowers | |
| OCT | plant | |
| NOV | / | |
| DEC | / | |

RECOMMENDED VARIETIES

*Viola wittrockiana:*

**Summer flowers**
  'Antique Shades'
  'Padparadja'
  'Romeo & Juliet'
  'Watercolours'

**Autumn/winter flowers**
  'Homefires'
  'Ultima Pastel Mixed'
  'Universal Mixed'
  'Velour Mixed'

## CONDITIONS

**Aspect**   Autumn/winter pansies need full sun. Summer flowering varieties like dappled shade.

**Site**   Add plenty of manure to the soil. Winter pansies need excellent drainage. Use multipurpose compost for containers.

## GROWING METHOD

**Sowing**   Sow from February under cover for flowers the same summer, or outside May–July for flowers the following spring. Either way, sow in a 9cm (3½in) pot of multipurpose compost and barely cover seeds. In early spring keep at 15°C (60°F) and transplant seedlings when large enough to cell trays, grow, harden off and plant in late May. When summer sowing, stand the pot outside in shade to germinate then treat seedlings the same, planting out in October where you want the plants to flower.

**Feeding**   Liquid feed summer plants fortnightly.

**Problems**   Spray with permethrin if aphids attack.

## FLOWERING

**Season**   Spring-sown plants flower in summer, autumn-sown from October onwards.

**Cutting**   Pansies last a few days in water.

## AFTER FLOWERING

**General**   Pull up and compost when finished.

# ZINNIA
## *Zinnia*

*ZINNIA FLOWERS tend to come as doubles but plants sometimes appear that are single like this. Zinnias are good bee plants.*

*IF PINCHED WHEN YOUNG zinnias make bushy, branching plants that fill gaps in mixed borders quickly. Take dead flowers off.*

## FEATURES

There is a zinnia for every garden. Dwarf varieties at 15cm (6in) tall are suited to beds and containers, while 'Dahlia-Flowered Mixed' has big heads on stems 60cm (2ft) high, and is useful for mixed borders. Modern varieties have fully double flowers, and some like 'Zebra Mixed' are stripey. 'Starbright Mixed' is an unusual variety with masses of small orange and gold flowers. Red, yellow, pink, scarlet, orange, lavender, purple, white and even green are typical flower colours. Half-hardy annual.

### ZINNIA AT A GLANCE

A half-hardy annual grown for its bright flowers in a wide range of colours, for bedding and cutting. Frost hardy to 0°C (32°F).

| | | |
|---|---|---|
| Jan | / | |
| Feb | / | |
| Mar | / | |
| Apr | / | |
| May | sow | |
| Jun | thin out | |
| July | flowering | |
| Aug | flowering | |
| Sept | flowering | |
| Oct | flowering | |
| Nov | / | |
| Dec | / | |

RECOMMENDED VARIETIES

**Zinnia hybrids:**
**Tall varieties**
 'Allsorts'
 'Dahlia-Flowered Mixed'
 'Zebra Mixed'
**Short varieties**
 'Belvedere'
 'Fairyland'
 'Persian Carpet Mixed'
 'Starbright Mixed'
 'Thumbelina'

## CONDITIONS

**Aspect**
**Site** Zinnias enjoy heat and need sun and shelter. Must have well-drained soil, previously improved with rotted organic matter. For containers use multipurpose compost.

## GROWING METHOD

**Sowing** Although half-hardy, zinnias grow best when sown direct where they are to flower, in short drills 1cm (½in) deep. Do this is in May and cover seedlings with a piece of garden fleece on frosty nights. Thin out seedlings so the young plants are eventually 15–60cm (6–24in) apart, depending on their final size. To grow dwarf varieties in containers sow 2–3 seeds to a 7.5cm (3in) pot at the same time, leave just the strongest, grow on, and plant when ready, not disturbing the roots.

**Feeding** Extra feeding is usually not necessary.
**Problems** Powdery mildew can be a problem, so avoid planting too close – sulphur sprays can help. Stem rots cause plants to collapse suddenly.

## FLOWERING

**Season** Flowers appear from midsummer onwards.
**Cutting** Very good cut flower. 'Envy Double' is a striking plant with double green flowers.

## AFTER FLOWERING

**General** Pull up in autumn and compost.

# CUTTING FLOWERS

*There is one point of view that annuals,*
*like all flowers, look best in the*
*garden, but we spend a lot of*
*time indoors and we can often best*
*enjoy our flowers there.*

An arrangement of fresh flowers will brighten a room, bringing inside the beauties of nature that otherwise are left at the door. Picking fresh flowers that you have planted and maintained over several months is one of the delights of gardening, but whether you are picking your own flowers or buying cut flowers, you will want to do all you can to get the best out of them and the longest vase life. These hints will help you achieve just that.

*LEFT: Harmony in contrast – huge yellow sunflowers and small blue cornflowers. Both will last five days or so in water.*

*ABOVE: The coneflower in close-up reveals its intricate structure.*

## PICKING FLOWERS

When picking flowers from your garden, do so early in the morning or late in the afternoon. Cool them quickly by placing them in a bucket of cool water in a cool place and leave them to absorb water for an hour or so. This is especially important in hot summer weather. After this initial soaking you can then arrange them at your leisure.

## BUYING CUT FLOWERS

If you are buying cut flowers, look for bright, fresh looking flowers that are just starting to open, and avoid flowers that have been standing in the sun or have been exposed to car exhaust fumes. Flowers with yellowing leaves on the stem or flowers with slimy stems have been in water for quite some time and are unlikely to be very satisfactory. When you get your flowers home, put them straight into a bucket of water without unwrapping them and leave them in a cool place to revive.

## HYGIENE

Make sure your vases are perfectly clean. Old stains in vases could be bacteria that will cloud the water, blocking uptake through the stems, causing flowers to wilt. Stains that are difficult to remove with normal washing-up procedures may be removed by filling the vase with water and adding a few drops of household bleach. Leave this to soak for a couple of hours, rinse the vase well and refill with clean water.

## CLEAN WATER AND 'FLOWER FOOD'

Clean water is vital for prolonging the life of cut flowers. You can change the vase water daily or use a cut flower food available from florists' shops. If you doubt that the effort or cost involved in using a preservative is worth while, test it for yourself by putting similar flowers in two separate vases. Add preservative to one vase and then leave the vases for a few days without changing the water. It won't be hard to tell the difference!

There are a number of very good preservatives on the market or you can make your own by combining 300ml of lemonade (not diet type), 300ml of water and half a teaspoon of household bleach. The sugar in the lemonade provides food for the flowers and the bleach kills off bacteria that would otherwise block the water-conducting tissues in the flower stem.

Check daily to see whether the water in the vase needs topping up or changing. Some flowers with woody stems drink a lot of water, especially in the first two or three days after cutting, and so need the water topped up each day.

### CENTAUREA
*Traditional favourites in red, pink, blue and white that can be used as a cut flower or hung up in bunches to dry for indoor decoration.*

### CAMPANULA

*Canterbury bells have large bell-like flowers on tall stems and are a good choice for early summer cutting, being sown the previous autumn and grown through the winter.*

### ZINNIA
*The stems of zinnias should be scalded after cutting to help them take up water. Pick when the flowers have begun to open but before the petals are fully expanded.*

### COSMOS
*Flowers well into the Autumn with delicate ferny foliage and long stems supporting single or bi-coloured blooms. The fluted petals of 'Seashells' are particularly fascinating.*

### PAPAVER
*Poppies make good cut flowers if picked when in bud. Plunge the ends of the stems into boiling water for about 20 seconds when first picked.*

### CONEFLOWER

*The coneflower is a very good cut flower but be sure to pick them when the flowers are fully formed but before the petals have separated out too much.*

### MATTHIOLA

*Stocks are excellent, highly-scented flowers for cutting. The stems should be scalded when first picked and be sure to change the water every few days.*

### RUDBECKIA

*Long-lasting, brightly coloured daisy flowers with a prominent central cone. They may be all yellow or suffused with red or even brown.*

### COREOPSIS

*Pick coreopsis when the flowers are fully formed but the petals are still firm.*

### HELICHRYSUM

*The most popular choice for drying. Cut them just before the petals unfold as they will open more as they age.*

### MOLUCCELLA

*Bells of Ireland is one of the most striking of all annuals to grow for use as a dried flower. The large green bracts turn pale olive-brown after drying and as they age.*

## ARRANGING FLOWERS

Before arranging flowers in the vase, cut off a couple of centimetres of stem with sharp secateurs and be sure to remove any leaves that would be below the water level in the vase. Any left on the stem will rot quickly and pollute the water.

Daffodils, jonquils and tulips should not be placed with other flowers immediately after cutting as their secretions can cause other flowers to collapse prematurely. Place them in a separate vase for a few hours before adding them to a mixed arrangement.

If flowers develop bent necks, that generally means they have an air lock in the stem and so are unable to absorb water properly. Recut the stems under water and place them in cool, deep water for at least a couple of hours before attempting to re-arrange them.

Most flower stems absorb water best if cuts are made between nodes or joints; this is certainly true of carnations and hydrangeas. In the past many people believed that hydrangeas and some other flowers would absorb water better if the base of the stem was crushed with a hammer. This crushed tissue will in fact block up very quickly with bacteria and prevent the flower from drawing up water. Sharp, clean cuts are to be preferred as they allow the stem to absorb water most efficiently.

A number of annuals respond well to having the stems scalded for a few seconds. Place the end of the stem in boiling water for about 20 seconds but do keep the heads out of the steam.

## MAKING THE MOST OF YOUR FLOWERS

Once the flowers are arranged in the vase, there are still a number of things you can do to make sure you get the best from them. For instance, cut flowers will not last well if you place the vase in full sun next to a window, or in rooms that are overheated. Strong draughts will also dry out cut flowers quite rapidly. And take care not to put vases of flowers next to your fruit bowl – the ripening fruit gives off ethylene, a natural ripening agent that ages flowers prematurely.

Be sure to remove individual flowers as they die. This will keep your arrangement looking attractive for much longer – mixed arrangements in particular can have their lives extended if the shorter lived flowers are removed.

Some cut flowers, especially daisies and stocks, will produce an unpleasantly strong smell as they age in the flower vase.

| PLANT NAME | SPRING | | | SUMMER | | | AUTUMN | | | WINTER | | |
|---|---|---|---|---|---|---|---|---|---|---|---|---|
| | EARLY | MID | LATE | EARLY | MID | LATE | EARLY | MID | LATE | EARLY | MID | LATE |
| Abutilon | | | | ✿ | ✿ | ✿ | ✿ | | | | | |
| Ageratum | | | | ✿ | ✿ | ✿ | ✿ | | | | | |
| Agrostemma | | | ✿ | ✿ | ✿ | ✿ | ✿ | | | | | |
| Alcea | | | | ✿ | ✿ | ✿ | ✿ | | | | | |
| Amaranthus | | | | ✿ | ✿ | ✿ | ✿ | ✿ | | | | |
| Antirrhinum | | | | ✿ | ✿ | ✿ | ✿ | | | | | |
| Arctotis | | | | ✿ | ✿ | ✿ | ✿ | | | | | |
| Begonia | | | | ✿ | ✿ | ✿ | ✿ | | | | | |
| Bellis | ✿ | ✿ | ✿ | | | | | | | | | ✿ |
| Brachyscome | | | | ✿ | ✿ | ✿ | | | | | | |
| Brassica | ✿ | ✿ | ✿ | | | | ✿ | ✿ | ✿ | ✿ | ✿ | ✿ |
| Browallia | | | | ✿ | ✿ | ✿ | ✿ | | | | | |
| Calceolaria | | | | ✿ | ✿ | ✿ | ✿ | | | | | |
| Calendula | | | | ✿ | ✿ | ✿ | ✿ | | | | | |
| Callistephus | | | | ✿ | ✿ | ✿ | ✿ | ✿ | | | | |
| Campanula | | | | ✿ | ✿ | ✿ | ✿ | | | | | |
| Catharanthus | | | | ✿ | ✿ | ✿ | ✿ | | | | | |
| Celosia | | | | ✿ | ✿ | ✿ | ✿ | | | | | |
| Centaurea | | | ✿ | ✿ | ✿ | ✿ | ✿ | | | | | |
| Chieranthus | ✿ | ✿ | | | | | | | | | | |
| Cleome | | | | ✿ | ✿ | ✿ | ✿ | | | | | |
| Consolida | | | ✿ | ✿ | ✿ | ✿ | ✿ | | | | | |
| Coreopsis | | | | | ✿ | ✿ | ✿ | ✿ | | | | |
| Cosmos | | | | ✿ | ✿ | ✿ | ✿ | | | | | |
| Dahlia | | | ✿ | ✿ | ✿ | ✿ | ✿ | | | | | |
| Delphinium | | | | ✿ | ✿ | ✿ | ✿ | | | | | |
| *Dianthus barbatus* | | ✿ | ✿ | ✿ | ✿ | | | | | | | |
| *Dianthus chinensis* | | | | ✿ | ✿ | ✿ | ✿ | | | | | |
| Digitalis | | | | ✿ | ✿ | | | | | | | |
| Dorotheanthus | | | | ✿ | ✿ | ✿ | ✿ | | | | | |
| Eschscholzia | | | | ✿ | ✿ | ✿ | ✿ | | | | | |
| Euphorbia | | | | ✿ | ✿ | ✿ | ✿ | | | | | |
| Gazania | | | | ✿ | ✿ | ✿ | ✿ | | | | | |
| Godetia | | | | ✿ | ✿ | ✿ | ✿ | | | | | |
| Gomphrena | | | | ✿ | ✿ | ✿ | ✿ | | | | | |
| Gypsophila | | | | ✿ | ✿ | ✿ | ✿ | | | | | |
| Helianthus | | | | ✿ | ✿ | ✿ | ✿ | | | | | |
| Helichrysum | | | | ✿ | ✿ | ✿ | ✿ | ✿ | | | | |
| Helipterum | | | | ✿ | ✿ | ✿ | ✿ | | | | | |
| Iberis | | | | ✿ | ✿ | ✿ | | | | | | |
| Impatiens | | | | ✿ | ✿ | ✿ | ✿ | ✿ | | | | |
| Ipomoea | | | | | ✿ | ✿ | ✿ | | | | | |
| Kochia | | | | ✿ | ✿ | ✿ | ✿ | ✿ | | | | |
| Lathyrus | | | | ✿ | ✿ | ✿ | ✿ | | | | | |
| Lavatera | | | | ✿ | ✿ | ✿ | ✿ | | | | | |

| PLANT NAME | SPRING | | | SUMMER | | | AUTUMN | | | WINTER | | |
|---|---|---|---|---|---|---|---|---|---|---|---|---|
| | EARLY | MID | LATE | EARLY | MID | LATE | EARLY | MID | LATE | EARLY | MID | LATE |
| Limnanthes | | | | ❀ | ❀ | | | | | | | |
| Limonium | | | | | ❀ | ❀ | ❀ | | | | | |
| Linaria | | | | | ❀ | ❀ | ❀ | | | | | |
| Lobelia | | | | ❀ | ❀ | ❀ | ❀ | | | | | |
| Lobularia | | | | ❀ | ❀ | ❀ | ❀ | | | | | |
| Lunaria | | | | ❀ | ❀ | ❀ | ❀ | | | | | |
| Lupinus | | | | ❀ | ❀ | ❀ | ❀ | | | | | |
| Malcolmia | | ❀ | ❀ | ❀ | ❀ | ❀ | ❀ | | | | | |
| Matthiola | | ❀ | ❀ | | | | | | | | | |
| Mimulus | | | | ❀ | ❀ | ❀ | ❀ | | | | | |
| Molucella | | | | ❀ | ❀ | ❀ | ❀ | | | | | |
| Myosotis | | ❀ | ❀ | | | | | | | | | |
| Nemesia | | | | ❀ | ❀ | ❀ | ❀ | | | | | |
| Nemophila | | | ❀ | ❀ | ❀ | ❀ | ❀ | | | | | |
| Nicotiana | | | | ❀ | ❀ | ❀ | ❀ | | | | | |
| Nigella | | | | ❀ | ❀ | ❀ | ❀ | ❀ | | | | |
| Osteospermum | | | | ❀ | ❀ | ❀ | ❀ | ❀ | | | | |
| *Papaver nudicaule* | | | ❀ | ❀ | ❀ | ❀ | ❀ | | | | | |
| *Papaver rhoeas* | | | ❀ | ❀ | ❀ | ❀ | ❀ | | | | | |
| Pelargonium | | | | ❀ | ❀ | ❀ | ❀ | | | | | |
| Petunia | | | | ❀ | ❀ | ❀ | ❀ | | | | | |
| Phlox | | | | ❀ | ❀ | ❀ | ❀ | | | | | |
| Portulaca | | | | ❀ | ❀ | ❀ | ❀ | | | | | |
| Primula | ❀ | ❀ | ❀ | | | | | | | | | ❀ |
| Ranunculus | ❀ | ❀ | ❀ | | | | | | | | | |
| Reseda | | | | ❀ | ❀ | ❀ | ❀ | | | | | |
| Ricinus | | | | ❀ | ❀ | ❀ | ❀ | | | | | |
| Rudbeckia | | | | ❀ | ❀ | ❀ | ❀ | | | | | |
| Salpiglossis | | | | ❀ | ❀ | ❀ | ❀ | | | | | |
| Salvia | | | | ❀ | ❀ | ❀ | ❀ | | | | | |
| Scabiosa | | | | ❀ | ❀ | ❀ | ❀ | | | | | |
| Schizanthus | | | | ❀ | ❀ | ❀ | ❀ | | | | | |
| Senecio | | | | ❀ | ❀ | ❀ | ❀ | ❀ | | | | |
| Solenostemon | | | | ❀ | ❀ | ❀ | ❀ | | | | | |
| Tagetes | | | | ❀ | ❀ | ❀ | ❀ | | | | | |
| Thunbergia | | | | ❀ | ❀ | ❀ | ❀ | | | | | |
| Tithonia | | | | ❀ | ❀ | ❀ | ❀ | | | | | |
| Torenia | | | | ❀ | ❀ | ❀ | ❀ | | | | | |
| Tropaeolum | | | | ❀ | ❀ | ❀ | ❀ | | | | | |
| Verbena | | | | ❀ | ❀ | ❀ | ❀ | | | | | |
| *Viola cornuta* | | ❀ | ❀ | ❀ | ❀ | ❀ | ❀ | | | | | |
| *Viola tricolor* | ❀ | ❀ | ❀ | ❀ | ❀ | ❀ | ❀ | | | | | |
| *Viola wittrockiana* | | ❀ | ❀ | ❀ | ❀ | ❀ | ❀ | ❀ | ❀ | ❀ | ❀ | ❀ |
| Zinnia | | | | ❀ | ❀ | ❀ | ❀ | | | | | |

# INDEX

## A

abutilon, 12, 106
*Abutilon pictum* 'Thompsonii', 12
African daisy, 18
African marigold, 92
ageratum, 13, 106
*Ageratum houstonianum*, 13
*Agrostemma githago*, 14, 106
*Alcea rosea*, 15
alyssum, 61
amaranthus, 16, 106
*Amaranthus caudatus*, 16
*Amaranthus cruentus*, 16
*Amaranthus hybridus*, 16
*Amaranthus tricolour*, 16
annual
    delphinium, 37
    lupin, 63
    mallow, 56
    phlox, 79
antirrhinum, 17, 106
*Antirrhinum majus*, 17
arctotis, 18, 106
*Arctotis hirsuta*, 18
*Arctotis hybrida*, 18
*Arctotis venusta*, 18
aster, China, 26

## B

baby blue eyes, 70
baby's breath, 47
balsam, 52
bedding dahlia, 36
bedding geranium, 76
begonia, 19, 106
begonia, trailing, 19
begonia, tuberous, 19
*Begonia semperflorens*, 19
bellis, 20, 106
*Bellis perennis*, 20
bells of Ireland, 67
black-eyed Susan, 93
Brachyscome, 21
*Brachyscome iberidifolia*, 21
Brassica, 22
Brompton stock, 65
browallia, 23, 106
*Browallia speciosa*, 23
burning bush, 54
bush violet, 23

busy lizzie, 52
buttercup, Persian, 82
butterfly flower, 89

## C

cabbage, ornamental, 22
calceolaria, 24, 106
calendula, 25, 106
*Calendula officinalis*, 25
California poppy, 42
*Callistephus chinensis*, 26
*Campanula medium*, 27
candytuft, 51
Canterbury bells, 27
castor oil plant, 84
*Catharanthus roseus*, 28
celosia, 29, 106
*Celosia argentea*, 29
*Celosia spicata*, 29
centaurea, 30, 106
*Centaurea cyanus*, 30
cheiranthus, 31, 106
*Cheiranthus cheiri*, 31
cineraria, see senecio
cleome, 32, 106
*Cleome spinosa*, 32
cockscomb, 29
coleus, 91
coneflower, 85
consolida, 33, 106
*Consolida ambigua*, 33
coreopsis, 34, 106
*Coreopsis tinctoria*, 34
*Coreopsis grandiflora*, 34
corncockle, 14
cornflower, 30
cosmos, 35, 106
*Cosmos bipinnatus*, 35
*Cosmos sulphureus*, 35
cypress, summer, 54

## D

dahlia, 36, 106
daisy, 20
    everlasting, 50
    Livingstone, 41
    swan river, 21
delphinium, 37, 106
*Delphinium grandiflorum*, 37

devil-in-a-bush, 72
dianthus, 38, 39, 106
*Dianthus barbatus*, 38
*Dianthus chinensis*, 39
digitalis, 40, 106
*Digitalis purpurea*, 40
dorotheanthus, 41, 106
*Dorotheanthus bellidiformis*, 42
dusty miller, 90

## E

Eschscholzia, 42, 106
*Eschscholzia californica*, 42
euphorbia, 43, 106
*Euphorbia marginata*, 43
everlasting daisy, 50

## F

flame nettle, 91
floss flower, 13
flowering chart, 106-107
flowering maple, 12
flowers
    arranging, 105
    buying, 104
    cutting, 103-105
    making the most of, 105
    picking, 104
    preserving water for, 104
forget-me-not, 68
foxglove, 40
French marigold, 92

## G

gazania, 44, 106
*Gazania rigens*, 44
geranium
    bedding, 76
    ivy-leaved, 76
globe amaranth, 46
godetia, 45, 106
gomphrena, 46, 106
*Gomphrena globosa*, 46
gypsophila, 47, 106
*Gypsophila elegans*, 47
*Gypsophila muralis*, 47

## H

heartsease, 99

helianthus, 48, 106
*Helianthus annuus*, 48
helichrysum, 49, 106
*Helichrysum bracteatum*, 49
helipterum, 50, 106
*Helipterum roseum*, 50
hollyhock, 15
honesty, 62

## I

Iceland poppy, 74
iberis, 51, 106
*Iberis umbellata*, 51
impatiens, 52, 106
*Impatiens balsamifera*, 52
ipomoea, 53, 106

## J

Johnny-jump-up, 99

## K

kale, ornamental, 22
kochia, 54, 106
*Kochia scoparia*, 54

## L

larkspur, 33
lathyrus, 55, 106
*Lathyrus odoratus*, 55
lavatera, 56, 106
*Lavatera trimestris*, 56
limnanthes, 57, 107
*Limnanthes douglasii*, 57
limonium, 58, 107
*Limonium sinuatum*, 58
linaria, 59, 107
*Linaria anticaria*, 59
*Linaria maroccana*, 59
*Linaria reticulata*, 59
Livingstone daisy, 41
lobelia, 60, 107
*Lobelia erinus*, 60
lobularia, 61, 107
*Lobularia maritima*, 61
love-in-a-mist, 72
love-lies-bleeding, 16
lunaria, 62, 107

*Lunaria annua*, 62
lupinus, 63, 107
*Lupinus luteus*, 63
*Lupinus texensis*, 63
*Lupinus varius*, 63

## M

Madagascar periwinkle, 28
malcolmia, 64, 107
*Malcolmia maritima*, 64
marigold, 92
African, 92
English, 92
French, 92
pot, 25
matthiola, 65, 107
*Matthiola incana*, 65
Mesembryanthemum, 41
Mexican sunflower, 94
mignonette, 83
mimulus, 66, 107
moluccella, 67, 107
*Moluccella laevis*, 67
money plant, 62
monkey flower, 66
morning glory, 53
myosotis, 68, 107
*Myosotis sylvatica*, 68

## N

nasturtium, 96
nemesia, 69, 107
*Nemesia strumosa*, 69
nemophila, 70, 107
*Nemophila insignis*, 70
*Nemophila maculata*, 70
*Nemophila menziesii*, 70
nicotiana, 71, 107
*Nicotiana sanderae*, 71
*Nicotiana langsdorfii*, 71
*Nicotiana sylvestris*, 71
nigella, 72, 107
*Nigella damascena*, 72
*Nigella orientalis*, 72

## O

orchid, poor man's, 89
ornamental cabbage, 22
ornamental kale, 22
osteospermum, 73, 107

## P

pansy, 100
summer, 100
autumn/winter, 100
papaver, 74, 75, 107
*Papaver nudicaule*, 74
*Papaver rhoeas*, 75
pelargonium, 76, 107
Persian buttercup, 82
petunia, 77, 78, 107
Milliflora, 77, 78
Multiflora, 77, 78
Floribunda, 77, 78
Grandiflora, 77, 78
*Petunia hybrida*, 77
phlox, 79, 107
*Phlox drummondii*, 79
pink, Chinese, 39
poached egg flower, 57
polyanthus, 81
poor man's orchid, 89
poppy
California, 42
Iceland, 74
Shirley, 75
portulaca, 80, 107
*Portulaca grandiflora*, 80
primula, 81, 107
Prince of Wales' feathers, 29

## R

ranunculus, 82, 107
*Ranunculus asiaticus*, 82
reseda, 83, 107
*Reseda odorata*, 83
ricinus, 84, 107
*Ricinus communis*, 84
rudbeckia, 85, 107
*Rudbeckia hirta*, 85

## S

sage, scarlet, 87
salpiglossis, 86, 107
*Salpiglossis sinuata*, 86
salvia, 87, 107
*Salvia splendens*, 82
scabiosa, 88, 107
*Scabiosa atropurpurea*, 88
*Scabiosa stellata*, 88
scabious, sweet, 88
scarlet sage, 87

schizanthus, 89, 107
*Schizanthus pinnatus*, 89
senecio, 90, 107
*Senecio cineraria*, 90
Shirley poppy, 75
slipper flower, 24
snapdragon, 17
snow-on-the-mountain, 43
solenostemon, 91, 107
*Solenostemon scutellarioides*, 91
spider flower, 32
statice, 58
stock
    Brompton, 65
    Virginian, 64
strawflower, 49
summer cypress, 54
sun plant, 80
sunflower, 48
    Mexican, 94
swan river daisy, 21
sweet pea, 55
sweet scabious, 88
sweet William, 38

## T

tagetes, 92, 107
*Tagetes tenuifolia*, 92
thunbergia, 93, 107
*Thunbergia alata*, 93
tickseed, 34
tithonia, 94, 107
*Tithonia rotundifolia*, 94
toadflax, 59
tobacco plant, 71
torenia, 95, 107
*Torenia fournieri*, 95
tropaeolum, 96, 107
*Tropaeolum majus*, 96

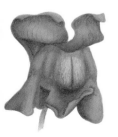

## V

verbena, 97, 107
*Verbena hybrida,* 97
viola, 98, 99, 100
*Viola cornuta*, 98, 107
*Viola tricolor*, 99, 107
*Viola wittrockiana*, 100, 107
violet, bush, 23
Virginian stock, 64

## W

wallflower, 31
wild pansy, 99
wishbone flower, 95

## Z

zinnia, 101, 107
*Zinnia elegans*, 101

Published by Merehurst Limited, 1998
Ferry House, 51-57 Lacy Road, Putney, London SW15 1PR



ISBN S403/1–85391–700–1

A catalogue of this book is available from the British Library.

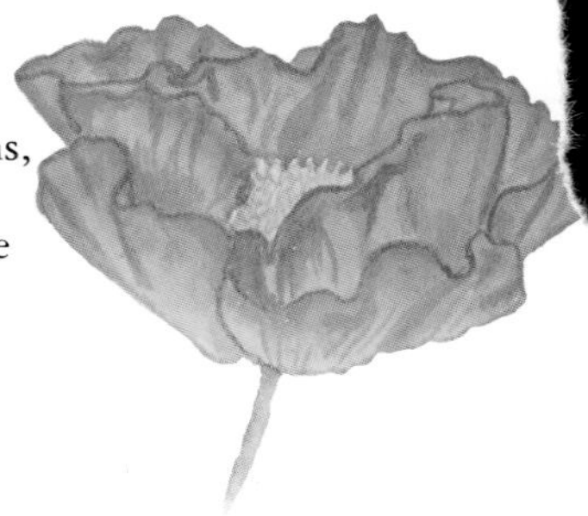

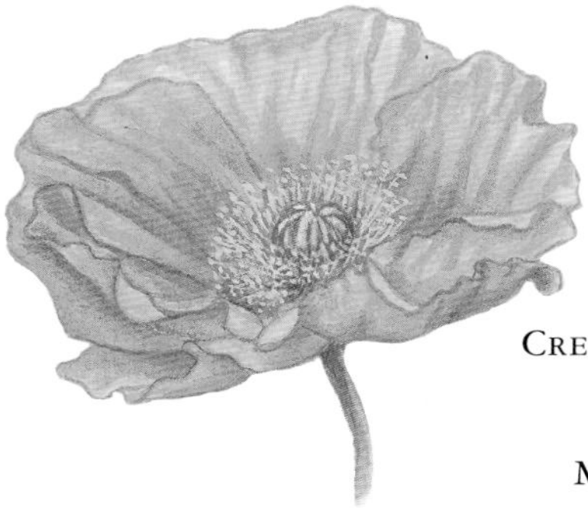

SERIES EDITOR: Graham Strong

EDITOR: John Walker

TEXT: Margaret Hanks

DESIGNER: Karen Awadzi

CREATIVE DIRECTOR: Marylouise Brammer

ILLUSTRATOR: Sonya Naumov

MANAGING EDITOR: Christine Eslick

COMMISSIONING EDITOR: Helen Griffin

PUBLISHER: Anne Wilson

PHOTOGRAPHS: All photographs by Lorna Rose except those by Gregory Lewis (pp86L and R, 89L): Stirling Macoboy (pp70L, 47, 46R, 45R, 59, 54R); Tony Rodd (pp34L and R); Graham Strong (pp8, 24R, 52R, 53, 68); Eric Sawford (pp21L and R, 71R, 84L, 93); Suttons (pp23, 27R, 36R, 52L, 76L and R, 77R, 81L and R, 98L and R); Mr Fothergill's (pp48R, 78 (bottom), 91R, 96L and R); Thompson & Morgan (p77L); John Walker (p78); Unwins (p91L).

FRONT COVER: Gazanias, a novel addition to any summer bedding scheme
TITLE PAGE: Delicate and fragrant, the sweet pea